FLOWERING SHRUBS

Step by Step to Growing Success

David Carr

CROWOOD GARDENING GUIDE

First published in 1991 by
The Crowood Press Ltd
Gipsy Lane
Swindon
Wiltshire SN2 6DQ

British Library Cataloguing in Publication Data

Carr, David, *1930–*
 Flowering shrubs.
 I. Title
 635.976

 ISBN 1 85223 505 5

Picture Credits
The photographs on pages 6(top), 7, 28, 41, 45, 46, 79, 81, 86, 87, 88,
89(bottom), 90, 91, 93, 95, 98(top), 102, 104, 105, 106, 107, 112, 113, 114, 115,
117, 118, 120(top), 121, 123 and 124 are reproduced courtesy of Dave Pike.
The other photographs in the book are reproduced courtesy of Natural
Image: pages 9, 14, 78, 89(top), 94, 98, 100, 103 and 127 by Robin Fletcher;
pages 4, 80, 82, 101, 110, 111, 120(bottom) and the frontispiece by Bob Gibbons; pages 6(bottom), 122 and 126 by Liz Gibbons; page 84 by Jean Hall;
and page 92 by Paul Davis.

All colour artwork by Claire Upsdale-Jones

Typeset by Avonset, Midsomer Norton, Bath
Printed and bound by Times Publishing Group, Singapore

Contents

CHAPTER 1

About Shrubs

This book is intended for all those with an interest in flowering shrubs– be it choosing, using or simply looking after them. The term 'flowering' is used in its widest context – some of the shrubs listed are grown mainly for their attractive foliage or stems, with the flowers being of secondary importance. However, without exception, all have garden merit. No more so than when well grown in a suitable setting.

The reader should note that some of the shrubs mentioned, when trained with a single trunk, may be found catalogued as small trees.

OBJECTIVES

It is probably true to say that the majority of shrubs sold at garden centres are bought on impulse because they look good at the time or are under promotional offer. All too often little or no real thought is given to their suitability for the garden in question. With this in mind, the aim here is to provide readers with the necessary information to enable them to select and grow shrubs successfully. As well as being a means of supplementing the advice given at the point of sale, which is at best usually sketchy, the book is also a useful back up to catalogues – which are of necessity little more than price lists. Meaningful yet comprehensive answers are given to the following fundamental questions:

1. Which shrubs are best suited to a given site?

Fig 1 As a choice summer flowering wall shrub, Fremontodendron Californicum deserves to be more widely planted – in all but the coldest sites.

2. Where should these shrubs be planted for maximum effect?
3. How should they be treated and cared for?

USING THE BOOK

When choosing shrubs for any location, first weigh up the local conditions (*see* Chapter 1). Then refer to Chapter 7 for the Plant Finder Guide and individual plant entries. Details, descriptions and uses of reliable popular flowering shrubs are given. These make up a comprehensive selection capable of providing year-round interest in the garden – with most soils, sites and situations catered for. Information on the various aspects of shrub care and cultivation are discussed systematically under the relevant chapters.

Newcomers to the shrub scene are advised to read through the book to get an overall picture. Thereafter, once experience is gained, the book will be found useful as a ready reference and memory jogger.

Details of heathers and heaths are given in another volume in the same series *Heathers and Conifers*.

USING SHRUBS

Although this book is primarily about choosing shrubs, their planting and aftercare, some reference to shrub use is unavoidable. This is because in practice, garden design and layout becomes so inextricably intertwined with shrub choice and care.

5

Fig 2   Fine textured shrubs provide a good foil
for statuary.

Cosmetic Effect

Few will argue that garden shrubs are planted as much for their appearance as for any other single consideration. A check list includes:-

Colour

The choice and combination of colours is largely a matter of personal preference. But when selecting shrubs for flower colour, do not overlook the possibilities fruit, foliage and bark have to offer as well. Where practical it is always a good idea to select double and multi-bonus shrubs which provide these foliage, fruit and bark colour effects in addition to flowers — very often maintaining colour interest for most of the year.

Fig 3   Abelia grandiflora *with its pink and white summer flowers is most attractive.*
It remains evergreen when grown against a warm wall in mild climates.

Fig 4 *A combination of colour and textural contrasts is provided by this planting of mixed shrubs.*

When thinking about colour schemes and themes it is important to keep in mind flowering times and season of colour. As a general rule foliage colour lasts longer than that of flowers. Compare for instance the foliage interest provided by *Weigela florida* 'Variegata' or *Elaeagnus pungens* 'Maculata' with the short but magnificent display of flowers from forsythia.

One important guideline which is truly worthy of note is the two to one rule. Plant two evergreens to every deciduous shrub or tree. This is a sound practice which helps to overcome winter bareness in the garden.

Texture

When selecting shrubs it is very easy to ignore foliage texture. A bad mistake — not only is there enormous scope here for variation but the texture of a shrub has a direct bearing on its usage. Look out for the small-leaved close-knit texture of the likes of *Hebe armstrongii* and clipped privet. Most dense textured shrubs are eminently suited to clipping for formal effects — individually or as hedgerows or as backdrops to beds and borders. At the other end of the scale comes the open-textured informality associated with the likes of artemisia and buddleia. These shrubs contrast well with the fine textured kinds in mixed borders, and broadly speaking they are more space demanding.

Habit

With flowering shrubs, the natural growth habit has very often been manipulated during training to suit various typical garden situations. For instance a trained standard *Buddleia alternifolia* or lilac makes an excellent specimen plant for the lawn or patio. Trained weeping standard *Cotoneaster* 'Hybridus Pendulus' and Wisteria are sometimes used for pool side planting where they reflect well in the water. And although *Forsythia suspensa* is usually sold as a free-standing bush it is also available part-trained as a wall plant.

Practical Benefits

While examining the practical benefits shrubs can contribute to a garden, never lose sight of their cosmetic influences. It is quite feasible to work the practical and cosmetic effects in together.

Fig 5 *Evergreen shrubs provide year-round colour and interest and combine comfortably with rock and border perennials.*

Camouflaging

Use wall plants and climbers to cover bare walls and down pipes; a container shrub to distract the eye from a conspicuous manhole cover; tall shrubs to blot out ugly views outside the garden; and climber-clad trellis to screen compost heaps, dustbins, coal bunkers and the like.

Physical Barriers

Consider medium and tall shrubs for formal hedging, or informal beds, borders and belts of planting. All will provide privacy and seclusion, or make effective enclosures. Strategically position-ed prickly and spiny shrubs are a deterrent to in-truders, but are not suitable where children might play. Try low growing ground cover shrubs to reduce the irritation of 'shortcutting' across open lawns. But be prepared to gather up litter which such plantings seem to attract from far and wide.

Shelter

Medium and tall shrubs with a minimum height of 5ft (1.5m), provide a most effective shelter from wind. A row of these shrubs, planted across the direction of oncoming wind, will protect plants and give shelter on the leeward side – up to a distance equal to five times their height. Wind-screens of shrubs filter and slow down air cur-rents, and in exposed gardens are to be recommended in preference to solid walls which cause damaging air turbulence within the garden.

Dust and Noise

Hedging and shrub screens, planted alongside noisy roads and thoroughfares lower the decibel level in the garden by absorbing and deflecting noise. By slowing down the windforce, any large particles of dust carried in the air stream stand a good chance of being deposited. Thus the dust content of the air within the garden is much reduced.

Micro-Climate

Shrubs can exert a marked influence on the climate within the garden. For instance, when shrubs are used as a windscreen they minimize the chilling factor of wind and have a warming effect.

In sunny gardens, large and medium sized sun-loving shrubs are often used to create a cool shaded spot – well suited to shade plants or for use as a sitting area. Elaeagnus and buddleia are suitable for the purpose. On a hot, sunny patio, if ground and walls are covered with vegetation the risk of excessive overheating is much reduced.

Shrubs like snowberry and tamarisk can be used to protect evergreens and spring flowering plants from frosting early in the year. Plants on east-facing sites are the most vulnerable. In a similar vein, a shrub canopy over choice subjects in the border will give some protection from radiation frost on clear spring nights.

Some long lived, slow growing plants like camellias and magnolias benefit from the pro-tection afforded by short lived quick growing plants planted alongside as a nurse crop. Brooms are popular nurse crops. Setting out nurse crops is sound practice, and of particular benefit in the establishment of more difficult shrubs.

Soil Stability and Erosion

Ground cover shrubs, along with others like low growing broom, cotoneaster and berberis – noted for their soil binding qualities – are fre-quently used to stabilize the soil on steep banks which are too difficult to mow if put down to grass. Plant across the slope and erosion by sur-face water run off is greatly reduced.

Shade

In mature gardens, with trees and hedges well grown, it is commonplace for ever increasing areas to become shaded unless drastic steps are taken. In many instances these shaded areas

Fig 6   Helianthemums – sun-roses – are renowned for their brilliant summer colour

are too dark for lawn grasses to grow. This is where shade tolerant shrubs come into their own. They make effective underplanting as an alternative to grass. And in so doing minimize the problem of moss in these locations. Periwinkle, euonymus and pachysandra are some of the best shrubs for underplanting in shade.

Economics

Shrubs, provided they are chosen wisely in the first place, need minimal maintenance and care in terms of both time and money. When well established, dense ground cover shrubs make good weed smother, which is again laboursaving. Permanent plantings of shrubs, in a tastefully laid out and well maintained laboursaving garden, will undoubtedly enhance the value of almost any property.

Conservation and Wildlife

In a conservation conscious era it is desirable, and indeed relatively easy, to combine conservation and a consideration for wildlife, with your gardening.

Flowering and berrying shrubs, for example, can be carefully chosen to provide shelter and food for butterflies, and benefitting insects and birds without interfering with the enjoyment of the garden.

PLANTING POLICY

Do not be too hasty in your enthusiasm to go out and buy shrubs. First weigh up what effect is wanted from the garden and what is the best way to achieve the desired results.

9

Instant and Long-Term Effects

In most new gardens, shrubs are planted out with the aim of getting immediate results – creating a mature garden as quickly as possible. This is highly commendable, but there is a price to pay in terms of effort and expense. There are several ways of tackling the job:

Use of Older Plants

It takes most young shrubs several years to reach their full maturity in terms of size and colour. Admittedly in the interim, the majority will put on a modest show – within a year or two of planting. One of the more obvious ways of obtaining instant effects is to set out larger, older and more mature plants. However, these are not always easy to get hold of. Some garden centres and nurseries do carry a limited range of what are variously called 'advanced' or 'extra heavy' stock – shrubs and trees which have been containerized and grown on for a few years. Because of the increased cost of labour and materials involved, expect to pay at least double or treble the price of 'standard nursery stock'. In addition to the initial outlay there are hidden extras to take into account. Larger shrubs take more handling to transport home; they take longer to plant out, and it is heavy work; they are at risk from root injury when planting out and a reasonable level of expertise is called for; and they may suffer a setback so adequate aftercare is vital. Nevertheless, 'advanced' or 'extra heavy' stock can give excellent results provided good plants are obtained in the first place and they are properly handled and cared for.

Shrubs are likely to suffer least setback – other things being equal – if planted out at the 'standard nursery stock size'.

Quick Maturing Varieties

Planting out quick maturing, rapidly growing varieties would seem to be yet another way to achieve a mature garden in a short space of time.

However, a few words of caution are called for. It is often the case that quick maturing shrubs also have a short lifespan and die out within a few years, requiring replacement. Brooms are a typical example. This problem apart, to limit the selection of shrubs to quick growers is to severely curtail choice and interest and is not to be recommended. Since the converse of quick growing, short lived shrubs is often also true – longer lived plants are frequently slow growers – the ideal is to plant a mixture of quick and slower growing kinds. In this situation, be ever mindful of the need to prevent the quick growers from taking over and permanently damaging the slow developers in the early days.

Plant Spacing

A bare-looking soil is to be expected if young shrubs are planted out in beds and borders at the spacings recommended on the label. To allow for growth and development, these spacings are normally calculated as being about three-quarters of the shrub's ultimate spread. To avoid expanses of bare soil, a common temptation is to set shrubs out much closer together. This is alright within reason, and provided there is selective thinning out of surplus shrubs in good time. Unfortunately, human nature being what it is, there is a natural reluctance to grub out healthy shrubs nearing the peak of their glory as being a needlessly wasteful practice. Invariably the result is overcrowding and spoiling after a few years. One of the best ways is to use temporary fillers resulting in 'phased obsolescence'. Plant out long-term shrubs at their correct spacings, then interplant with short lived shrubs, herbaceous perennials or annual bedding plants in due season. As the permanent shrubs grow and take over, so the temporary fillers are done away with.

Laboursaving or Work-Intensive Planting

The fussiness or otherwise of the actual layout and arrangement of a garden obviously has a direct bearing on the amount of time and effort needed to keep it in good order. The choice of shrubs likewise can be laboursaving or work generating. Aucuba and hebe are, for example, easy to care for, but the likes of buddleia, ligustrum and wisteria need more attention. But, for ease of future maintenance and success, perhaps the most important point of all to watch is to choose varieties which are suited to the existing site, soil and climate. To try to grow shrubs which will inevitably outgrow their allotted space unless restrained, or which need very differing conditions to those prevailing, is to invite trouble. A lot of extra work, expense and know-how are involved, and the outcome is still something of a gamble. By all means attempt to grow an odd favourite shrub irrespective of site. But view it as a calculated risk.

Shrub Choice and Site

The best garden design schemes are of little use unless the plants included in the layout grow and flourish. Before planting, try to anticipate the likely success — will the chosen shrubs do well in their proposed setting? Otherwise you risk disappointment and lost time. To plant up a shrub and wait three or five years for it to reach maturity is bad enough. But it is infuriating if, when it starts flowering, the flowers are frosted and killed off each year — simply because it blooms too early for the prevailing harsh weather.

Many disappointments can be avoided by taking time and trouble to weigh up the site conditions. Although the oft-quoted advice of asking neighbours, local garden centres, nurseries and horticultural societies is a useful starting point, it does not guarantee success. Take note which shrubs do well in the district but realize the limitations of doing so. It is a well established fact that within quite short distances — even within the same garden — variations can be quite dramatic and often make the difference between success and failure. For example, a marginally hardy shrub may grow along happily for years

when given the protection of a warm wall. But the same variety, if planted say 6ft(1.8m) out from the wall may well succumb to winter frost and wind. Planting climbers and wall shrubs close up to a warm wall affords a considerable degree of protection.

In chapter 7 details of the needs of individual shrubs are given. These requirements should be matched with the prevailing site conditions to assess the probability of success.

Hardiness

Hardiness is all about a plant's ability to survive and grow outdoors throughout the year. For instance, shrubs which are hardy in mild climates may not survive the rigours of hard winters.

In this book a system of hardiness rating has been adopted whereby shrubs which normally survive winter temperatures of 5 to 10°F (−15 to −12°C) are rated H1. Those which are hardy in open sites or in sheltered sites surviving winter temperatures of 10 to 20°F (−12 to −7°C) are rated H2. Shrubs listed as H3 are hardy only in sheltered positions, surviving winter temperatures of 20 to 30°F (−7 to −1°C).

Another important consideration related to climate and hardiness is the length of the growing season. This is largely determined by the length of the frost-free period between spring and autumn. Growth virtually ceases at about 42°F(5°C) and below. As a rough rule of thumb, spring is delayed by 7−10 days at sea level for every 100 miles(160km) further north travelled. As it is for each 300ft(91m) increase in altitude above sea level.

In areas with a limited growing season — cold winters and short summers — the climate tends to favour the growing of late spring or early summer flowering, fruiting and berrying shrubs. This is the reason these shrubs, along with those grown for their summer foliage, frequently dominate northern gardens. In the north, winter and early spring blooming kinds are vulnerable to frosting, while their flowers are at risk from wind damage. In the case of fruiting and berrying shrubs which flower early in frosty weather, displays are often poor because pollination and fruit set are hampered. Late summer and early autumn flowering shrubs, which flower on the current season's shoots, need a long frost-free period. These shrubs are at a disadvantage in short summer climates and are best reserved for areas with longer summers.

Exposure and Aspect

The question of shelter and the chilling effect of direct exposure to wind has already been touched upon – *see* page 8.

Spaces between buildings act as cold wind tunnels which are very damaging to plants.

When looking at the shelter factor it is also important to look at the closely related effect of aspect, effects of which are compounded on sloping ground, banks, walls and fences.

A south or west-facing aspect, provided that it is not shaded from sun by tall trees or buildings, is likely to be warmer than positions facing east or north. Other things being equal, southern aspects are the warmest and sunniest, followed by western, then eastern. Both west and east aspects are shaded for part of the day. A northern aspect is usually cold and sunless.

East-facing sites – walls in particular – invariably prove treacherous to late winter and spring flowering shrubs and evergreens. In these positions the danger is that early morning sun, after overnight frost, will bring about an over-quick thaw with consequential damage to buds, flowers and evergreen foliage. In these east-facing beds opt for later flowering deciduous shrubs, wall shrubs and climbers.

Sunlight and Shade

It is a relatively easy matter to note which parts of the garden are in full sun, partial shade or full shade, and to choose plants accordingly.

When planting in shade – as against a north wall – give plants a bit more space than when planting in reasonable light. This minimizes the risk of plants growing tall, weak and spindly. Do not plant directly under the branches of dense evergreen trees. No shrub will tolerate indefinitely the type of permanent heavy shade they cast.

Space to Grow

A very common failing among gardeners is to try to squeeze too much into too small an area. The result is inevitable – a jungle of tall, leggy plants which have outgrown their allotted space. In an effort to obtain light and air, in competition one with another, they reach for the sky. Below ground there is also a life and death struggle taking place, as the roots of one plant compete with those of its neighbour for any available nutrients and moisture. In consequence no plant is seen at its best. Slow growers are likely to be smothered out by the rampant kinds and in extreme cases, less vigorous varieties are killed off. As all are increasingly weakened by the unacceptably high levels of competition, pests, diseases and disorders become widespread. The whole question of space is particularly important with evergreens, because overcrowding results in loss of foliage and bare stems.

So, when organizing potential plantings, take time to measure the ground area as well as the available height and space above soil level. Armed with this information, it is a relatively simple matter to calculate fairly accurately how many permanent shrubs can be accommodated. Do not ignore any existing plants on site, but make allowances for their future. Information on the likely ultimate shrub size is available under individual plant entries in chapter 7.

The Soil

The soil exerts an enormous influence over the health and growth of shrubs, and while many excellent garden shrubs do grow satisfactorily on a wide range of soils, some varieties have very definite likes and dislikes. The best known and most often quoted examples to illustrate this point are rhododendrons and azaleas. When grown on alkaline or lime-rich soils these plants suffer from chlorosis – a yellowing of leaves and a stunting of growth.

Soil is a bit more tricky to assess than factors of site and climate. Nevertheless it is still advisable to try. Failure to find out something about conditions below ground prior to planting is to risk costly mistakes.

It is worth considering for a moment just what shrubs, and other plants, actually need from the soil. The most obvious necessities are adequate moisture, nutrients, air and warmth – in the right amounts and at the right time. Slightly less obvious is the need for secure plant anchorage – a good roothold, space to grow and develop, plus freedom from pollution.

Soil Depth

Most shrubs require a minimum 1–1½ft (30–45cm) depth of good topsoil. The taller the shrub the greater is the depth needed. Digging down vertically with a spade and examining the profile, will quickly give some answers in this respect. In reasonable garden soils expect to find a layer of dark, fertile topsoil overlying the paler, less fertile subsoil.

One very important aspect of topsoil depth is that the greater the depth, the greater is the drought resistance of shrubs growing in it. Fertile topsoil can be likened to a reservoir. The greater its depth the greater its reserves of moisture and nutrients.

Panning

Occasionally, the soil may be compacted and hard just below, or even at, the surface. This is particularly troublesome in new housing developments and is known as panning. It is commonly caused by building operations, but simply trampling on over-wet soil can have a similar effect. These hard pans prevent effective drainage and root development is inhibited. Sometimes, especially on chalk and limestone soils, a hard pan develops because of chemical action.

Soil Type and Texture

Soils are made up of a preponderance of mineral particles, plus organic matter, soil, air and water. The range is extensive, from sticky clays at one extreme, to coarse, gritty sands and stony or gravelly soils at the other. It is fairly easy, even for a relative newcomer, to identify a stiff, heavy clay soil. Wet a small sample of soil and squeeze it between finger and thumb. If it is clay it will feel greasy and smear readily. Do a similar test with sandy soil and it will feel gritty and soon rub off. There are a whole range of soils between these two extremes – containing varying amounts of fine particled clay and coarse grained sand. Such soils are normally referred to as loams and are amongst the most desirable and easiest to manage. The significance of establishing the clay and sand content of a soil is to get an idea of its likely behavioural pattern. Clay soils are difficult to work. They are sticky, intractable and easily puddled when wet. They set like concrete when they dry out – often leaving large surface cracks. Clay soils have notoriously poor drainage and water is slow to get away after heavy rain. These soils are also slow to warm up in spring. However, with good management they are amongst the richest and most fertile, containing ample reserves of plant nutrients. Sandy soils are normally easy to work. They drain readily but dry out badly in periods of prolonged drought. Light sandy soils are naturally low in nutrients and benefit from generous feeding and manuring. These soils tend to be somewhat weedy. However, on the credit side, they do warm up quickly in spring.

Chalk and limestone soils are also usually fairly easy to detect. If, when making an exploratory dig, the soil becomes progressively paler – changing to a dirty cream, even white at subsoil level – suspect chalk or limestone. Apply the same test as for clay and the sample will probably feel pasty if a high percentage of chalk or limestone is present. Clematis very often naturalizes in the hedgerows which is another clue. But the irrefutable test for chalk and limestone soils is to calculate its lime content by using a simple DIY soil test kit. Chalk and limestone soils bring about yellowing in the leaves of camellias, some magnolias as well as rhododendrons and azaleas. In common with sandy soils, chalky soils tend to be weedy and naturally low in nutrients.

Fen, peaty or moss soils make up the last of the extreme soil types. These are usually dark in colour and spongy to the touch. They contain large proportions of decayed mosses, sedges and grasses. They hold moisture and are slow to drain. Some are very acid and ideal for lime

Fig 7 Exploit the feathery texture and flower colour of Perovskia atriplicifolia *with bold yellow or pink flowers. It is especially good on alkaline soils.*

haters. These soils can support a wide range of shrubs provided they are limed and drained as necessary.

Lime and Acidity

In established gardens the existing vegetation can provide clues as to the likely lime content of the soil. For instance, healthy camellias, azaleas, heathers and rhododendrons are indicative of acid soils with a low level of lime. Box, clematis, iris, pinks and dianthus grow happily and flourish on lime-rich alkaline soils.

When taking over a new garden, it is sound practice to establish the lime content – pH – before planting shrubs. pH is a numerical scale, used by scientists and gardeners alike to measure 'potential hydrogen' levels – commonly referred to as the acidity or alkalinity of the soil. The scale goes from 1 to 14. A pH of 7 indicates the soil is more or less neutral. Below 7 the soil is acid, above 7 the soil is alkaline. In practice garden soils vary from very acid with a pH of 4.5 to alkaline with a pH of 8.5–9. The vast majority of shrubs, a few alkaline lovers excepted, grow well within the pH range 5.5–6.5.

Although soil samples can be tested in a laboratory, a simple DIY soil test kit is accurate enough for most practical purposes. Full instructions are supplied with the kits, as well as a table of application rates for liming to correct acidity. Follow the makers' recommendations closely and be aware that the way the samples are taken is a very important part of the operation. Take several samples of soil from the actual, or intended, root zones at about 6in(15cm) deep.

Lime is usually applied in winter in the form of ground limestone which consists entirely of calcium salts. However, dolomite products, which contain magnesium as well as calcium salts, are making their way increasingly onto the market and can be used to replace ground limestone when growing shrubs. To maintain fertility, an average routine dressing would be a handful of ground limestone per sq yd (m) [approx 4oz(120gm)]. Increase the dressing by half as

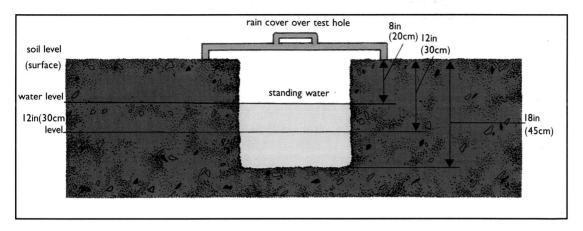

Fig 8   *The standing water test. When the water level rises to within 12in(30cm) of the surface, the land needs draining.*

much again when using dolomite limestone, and adjust the dressings to comply with the results of any soil test. Do not apply lime to land which is to grow lime haters – nor to chalky or limestone soils.

Soil Moisture and Drainage

Establish if the soil is well-drained before setting out shrubs rather than afterwards. With heavy clay soils there is always a danger of waterlogging – particularly on low lying land or in areas of high rainfall. In waterlogged soil it is inevitable that plant roots, standing in water for long periods, will suffocate and drown – with the death of the plant soon to follow. Wet, though not necessarily waterlogged, soils also bring their problems. They are cold, slow to warm up and favour diseases like root rots.

If in doubt about drainage, a simple but effective method of checking is the 'standing water' test. This test is best carried out in autumn or winter. It involves digging out a hole about 1½ft(45cm) across and of a similar depth, and then covering it over with a dustbin lid or slab of wood to keep out the rain. Inspect the hole after heavy rain or during periods of prolonged wet weather and note the level of standing water. If the water level has risen to within 1ft(30cm) – or less– of the surface, the land needs draining – *see* chapter 2.

It is also advisable to check the garden for dry spots, bearing in mind that these are potential death traps for moisture loving shrubs. Gardens most at risk are those on sandy soils during long, hot, dry summers. Positions at the top of banks, or on south-facing slopes, or at the foot of a warm wall are all highly suspect when it comes to drying out. Pay particular attention to the base of walls. Walls tend to act like wicks, sucking moisture out of nearby soil. Subsequently the moisture evaporates from the surface of the wall and is lost into the atmosphere.

Soil Fertility

Unfortunately, there is no simple yardstick for measuring soil fertility. But good cultivation, feeding, manuring, mulching and watering are all aids towards raising or maintaining fertility, while negative factors like pollution, pests and diseases all operate against fertility. From the standpoint of assessment, it is quite feasible to make a judgement based on the state of the vegetation. In the absence of plants it is much more difficult to say what the level of soil fertility is likely to be.

Soil Pollution

Pollution can arise from such basic things as spillage of oil or fuel, detergent from car washing, and salt spray from roads in winter. Soot and grime deposits in towns and industrial areas are regular hazards. Look at the proximity of planting

15

areas to these potential sources of trouble and act accordingly, choosing pollution resistant shrubs where necessary. Similarly note any dead or diseased vegetation and deal with it – see chapter 2.

The Shrubs

Many disappointments lie firmly at the door of paying insufficient attention to the whole question of buying in, and raising, shrubs. When buying shrubs, do not leave things until the last moment. This can result in having to make do with a second choice of variety, second-rate shrubs, end of season dregs, or missing a season's planting.

Traditionally, shrub planting is carried out in autumn or early winter when the new season's supply of young shrubs start coming into retail outlets. Ordering in good time and buying early in the season, helps to ensure that the pick of varieties and best quality plants are available. As the season progresses popular as well as 'new' varieties are sold out. Aim to have shrubs at the ready so that they can be set out during the planting season, as and when the weather and soil are suitable.

Autumn and early winter are recognized as the best times to plant out deciduous shrubs – once they have dropped their leaves. At this time of year the soil is still warm, and this encourages new roots to develop and goes a long way towards rapid and successful establishment. Evergreens are traditionally planted out during early autumn or spring, and these are still the best times of year to deal with the job.

Nowadays most shrubs are sold in containers, and they are usually worth the extra cost. Containerizing has influenced shrub planting by extending the season beyond traditional planting times. Both evergreen and deciduous plants can be set out during mild spells between early autumn and late spring with reasonable expectation of success. Withhold planting, however, during the heat of midsummer.

In cold exposed gardens, and where the soil is a wet, heavy clay, planting is best delayed until spring.

Bought-In or Home-Raised Plants

When starting a garden 'buying in' ready to plant shrubs is the obvious answer. This shortens the time lag between planting and having colour in the garden. Raising plants, by whatever means, takes several years in most cases. And there is always the problem of obtaining cuttings, suckers or layers (see chapter 5). When propagating shrubs a certain amount of skill and know-how is called for. This fact together with the ongoing attention to detail, and specialist equipment needed, often adds up to too much effort for the average gardener. However, there is no reason why the shrub enthusiast should not undertake raising replacements – once experience is gained and where there is not the same urgency.

Checklist of Points to Watch when Buying Shrubs

Value for Money

Shop around and compare prices and quality.

Labelling

Make sure the name on the label corresponds exactly with that on the shopping list. For instance *Cotoneaster dammeri* forms a carpeting shrub up to lft(30cm) high while *Cotoneaster* 'Cornubia' makes a tree of up to 20ft(6m) in height.

Shrub Suitability

Never be tempted to buy on impulse or accept substitute varieties unless absolutely sure that the shrub in question is suitable for the intended site and soil.

Shrub Appearances

Choose a sturdy, healthy, well-grown shrub of pleasing appearance. Note the size and condition having regard for the time of year. Deciduous shrubs are dormant and leafless in winter – a good time to assess balance and shape of bare branches. Young shrubs in leaf should have foliage evenly distributed over their stems, and down to compost level. When buying unfamiliar shrubs be aware that the flower and foliage colour may change with age, as can plant habit, leaf form and shape. The juvenile form of some shrubs can be very different from the mature adult, for example, with some hollies – they have prickly young leaves and smooth old ones. The first formed flowers on some young camellias may be single, small and pale. In a year or two the later blooms may be fully double and strongly coloured.

Root Condition

Ideally buy container-grown plants – they suffer minimum disturbance on moving. Some shrubs such as brooms and wisterias resent root disturbance to such an extent that they are difficult to establish unless container raised. Also, as already mentioned, container-grown shrubs allow for a greater flexibility in planting times, and they enable larger, more mature plants to be moved with a reasonable degree of safety. Look for well rooted plants, with a good balance of roots to top growth, and which are well anchored in the container. Those showing significant signs of movement may have only recently been potted, with insufficient time to become established and settle down. Such plants are likely to need nursing along after planting out. In the case of lifted, field-grown stock, avoid shrubs with dried-out, exposed roots. And think twice before buying uncontainerized plants out of season. To risk repetition, autumn is the season to set these plants out causing minimal disturbance and setback. Be on guard for signs of neglect such as:

1. Weedy and moss covered compost.
2. Pot-bound plants in small containers (with a large amount of top growth, exposed surface roots, or thick roots growing into the ground beneath the container).
3. Dried out compost shrinking back from the sides of the container.
4. Topgrowth – steer clear of puny, undersized shrubs, and of large, straggly and overgrown plants. When buying part-trained shrubs, for example in the case of standards, fan and espalier forms, look for a basic, well formed and balanced framework of branches.
5. Tall, weak and spindly shrubs with evidence of bare stems.
6. Wilted, scorched, discoloured, eaten or distorted leaves will mean pest and disease ridden plants.
7. Physical injury.
8. Reverted green shoots on variegated plants.
9. Unseasonal, premature or forced growth.
10. Windblown, scorched plants standing in draughty doorways or passageways.

Taking Delivery of Shrubs

Before transporting shrubs home, be sure to wrap up (in plastic sheet or fine mesh netting) any that are in leaf, if they are to be transported in an open car boot. This minimizes the risk of leaf scorch and severe injury.

Fig 9   Trained shrub forms.

On getting plants home – or taking delivery of shrubs from away – unwrap them immediately, water if dry, and stand in a sheltered spot until needed for planting.

In the event of mail order shrubs being delivered in hard frosty weather, place them in a cool, frost-free shed or garage. Remove the packing around the crown to allow a good circulation of air. Keep the roots moist and covered until the mild weather returns.

CHAPTER 2

Preparation and Planting

To provide a clear-cut, step by step routine in preparation for shrub planting is out of the question. So much depends on individual circumstances. Planting the odd shrub in a well managed garden requires minimal effort. Making a new garden from scratch is a vastly different undertaking — as it is to carry out major improvements to any existing layout.

WORK PROGRAMME

Organize the work systematically and much time and effort can be saved. Consider first the siteworks — clearance, tree surgery, building and construction work. Then deal with the groundwork — preparing the ground in readiness for planting. Finally prepare the plants.

Sitework

Nowadays, in new housing developments, much of the initial sitework (such as tree lopping and construction work) is carried out in advance of the new owners moving in. However, where old and neglected gardens are to be given a major facelift, quite drastic measures are likely to be needed. Work to a planned programme. A checklist might include:

1. Cut back and remove weeds, unwanted surface vegetation and rubbish.
2. Carry out any necessary remedial lopping, pruning and training of existing trees, shrubs and climbers. This is not only to render them safe but to let light and air into the garden and make more space. Grub out any that are dead or have outlived their useful life.
3. Make good any existing tree and climber supports.
4. Repair unsound structures, buildings, walls and fencing — paying particular attention to those near proposed planting areas.
5. Erect new buildings, sheds and greenhouses, free-standing and retaining walls, and fencing. Give priority to jobs in the vicinity of the planting areas. See to wind and shelter screens at the same time. With these and other construction works, carefully excavate and retain any good topsoil for future use.
6. Lay any new paths, driveways, paving and hard surfaced patio areas.
7. Put up supports for wall shrubs and climbers.

Supporting Wall Shrubs and Climbers

All too often supports for wall shrubs and climbers are hastily improvized and inadequate for their purpose. Basic requirements are that they are pleasing to the eye; and that they are strong enough to be reliably safe at all times — capable in fact of supporting the weight of fully mature plants under the worst possible weather of driving wind, rain and snow. Supports should be erected in such a way that the supporting walls are not weakened or damaged in the process.

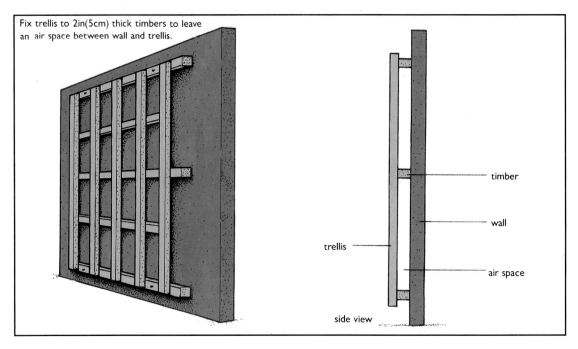

Fig I0   Trellis shrub support.

With a lengthy lifespan and future maintenance in mind, use rot-proof or corrosive-free materials. Treated timber, galvanized or plastic coated wire (or plastics) are all suitable. Pressure treated timber requires less maintenance than painted wood. When buying supports, relate purchase price to subsequent maintenance expenses to get a true picture.

Supports should be capable of being fixed so that an air space of about 2in(5cm) can be left between the trellis and the supporting wall (*see* Fig I0). Some climbers cling to masonry and brickwork by means of aerial roots and sucker pads — ivy, climbing hydrangea and parthenocissus are notable in this respect. In time they can cause extensive damage to buildings, particularly old ones, unless prevented from doing so by maintaining a clear air space between climber and wall. However, regardless of the type of climber or wall plant involved an air space is strongly recommended. The increased air flow reduces the risk of trapped moisture and consequential penetrating damp.

Relate the shape and nature of the support to the habit and type of plants being grown.

Possible types of support are free-standing arches, pergolas, pillars, trellis panels, posts and rails, and wire frames — these are the main supports in common use. Other alternatives are wall or fence-mounted trellis, wire or plastic rigid mesh, pliable netting, and wires and eyelets.

Fig II   Simple arch shrub support.

20

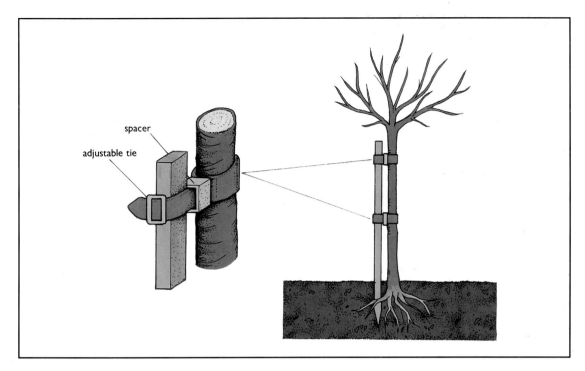

Fig 12   A stake and two ties for standard shrub support – one near the crown and one half-way down.

Groundwork

Success with shrubs depends to a large measure upon the thoroughness and efficiency of ground preparations prior to planting.

Builders normally leave gardens in a reasonable condition these days, with some of the initial jobs like levelling already completed. But again, as with sitework, where the aim is to carry out major improvements to an existing garden,

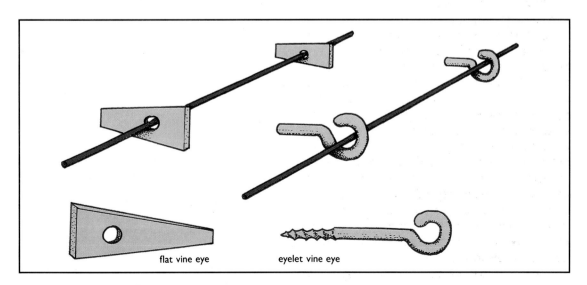

flat vine eye   eyelet vine eye

Fig 13   Wire and wall-fixing vine eyes for shrub support.

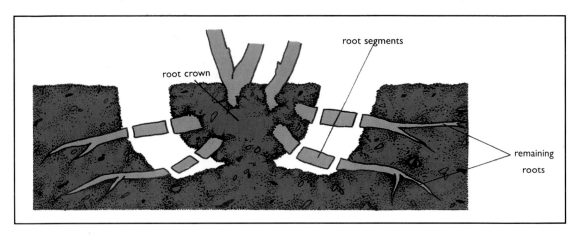

Fig 14 Grubbing out old roots. Systematically dig a circular trench around the root crown, severing and removing root segments. Lever out the main clump and finish by digging out remaining roots.

groundwork needs to be organized. When using the following checklist, think of it more as a memory jogger than something to be rigidly adhered to. Relate to individual circumstances – some of the jobs may not apply.

Grubbing Out

The best way to minimize the risk of root rots and various other problems being passed on to a new generation of shrubs, is to dig out old roots of redundant plants and weeds. In the case of border perennials and deep rooted persistent weeds, aim to fork out every bit of root.

Digging out sounds like a lot of hard work, but in the long term it is the quickest and safest approach. Choosing a time when the soil is dry enough to work in comfort, start to dig out a trench around the stump in question. Stack the topsoil to one side. A spade and pickaxe are good tools for the purpose. Take special care not to damage underground pipes and cables – they may be lying within 10–12in(25–30cm) of the surface. Saw or axe through each root as it is uncovered and exposed. Systematically work round the root clump, then winch or lever to ease it out. It is important to remove all the remaining pieces of severed root and they should come away quite easily. This helps to prevent carry-over of disease. Where there is any evidence of disease, drench with an approved

tar oil derivative or other suitable proprietary product.

Levelling

In the majority of gardens, little more than cultivating down high spots is needed and using the surplus topsoil to infill hollows. Never underestimate the importance of avoiding planting shrubs in low spots on clay soil, especially

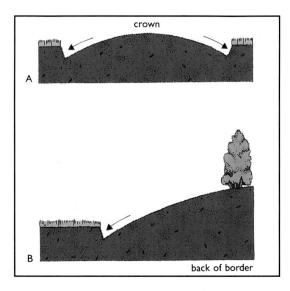

Fig 15 (A) The crown bed – rainwater is shed to the edges. (B) The high-back border – rainwater is shed to the front.

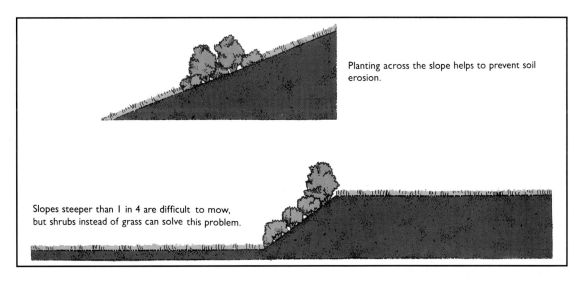

Planting across the slope helps to prevent soil erosion.

Slopes steeper than 1 in 4 are difficult to mow, but shrubs instead of grass can solve this problem.

Fig 16 Contour planting.

in areas of high rainfall. Shrubs set out in depressions of as little as 2in(5cm) below the surrounding soil are particularly at risk from waterlogging. In fact the merits of the age-old practice of planting on 'crown' beds and 'highback' borders still holds as good today as it ever did (see Fig 15). When dealing with sandy soils things are different. By planting shrubs in hollows, rain and irrigation water are held where needed.

Where slopes are steeper than 1 in 4, mowing grass often becomes something of a problem. Contour planting of shrubs across the slope can help (see Fig 16). On slopes steeper than 1 in 2½, if landslip and severe erosion are to be avoided, more drastic action is called for – usually in the form of terracing. This is a job for specialists though (see Fig 17).

When soil rests against a dwelling, ensure that it is kept at least 6in(15cm) below the level of the damp proof course.

Land Drainage

Broadly speaking there are three main contributory causes of poor drainage and water-

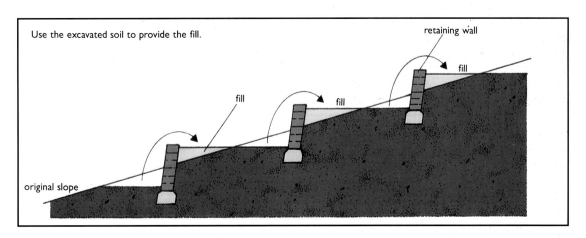

Use the excavated soil to provide the fill.

retaining wall

fill

fill

fill

fill

original slope

Fig 17 Terracing is a practical way to solve a slope problem, without the need to import or dispose of large amounts of earth.

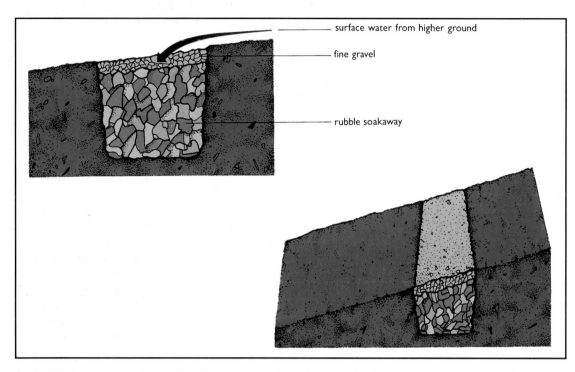

Fig 18   The French or Interceptor drain. Be sure to run the drain across the slope.

logging. The first is where subsoil water cannot get away quickly enough, often at its worst on low lying ground. In extreme cases the land is liable to flooding. The second major problem comes about when surface water is unable to percolate down through the topsoil to the sub-soil, which is a problem associated with clay soils of poor fertility – or less frequently with panning (*see* page 13). Finally a fairly common source of trouble is flood water draining off nearby higher ground, buildings and hard surfaced areas.

Rubble sump drains help to dispose of subsoil drainage water. In gardens it is neither practical nor indeed desirable to install full drainpipe systems, or to use open ditches. Pipe systems are costly and disruptive to install. Open ditches are a hazard to young children, they collect weeds, rubbish and flies, they get blocked and need regular attention. In both cases the lack of a suitable drainage outlet to a deep ditch or water course limits the feasibility of such a scheme in most residential areas.

One of the most practical solutions is to build one or more rubble sumps or soakaways. Expect each one to drain an area of up to about 20ft(6m) square – though obviously a lot depends on prevailing conditions. Having selected a low, badly drained spot, dig out a hole about 2½ft(75cm) square and approx 3ft(90cm) deep, stacking the topsoil to one side. Using clean builder's rubble, and consolidating as filling proceeds, part fill the hole, to within 1ft(30cm) of the top. Cover the rubble with a generous 1½in(4cm) layer of gravel before levelling off with good topsoil. The gravel reduces the problem of soil being washed down into the builder's rubble to render it less efficient.

French drains make useful interceptors to stem the flood of drainage water from adjoining high ground, sheds, buildings, large expanses of paved areas and pathways. In some instances they can also be used to speed up the percolation of water down through the soil. French drains are in effect rubble-filled trenches of about 1½ft(45cm) deep by about 1ft(30cm) wide, and topped over with gravel. When strategically positioned they can be most effective (*see* Fig 18).

Improving soil texture is normally the most

24

effective way to increase the rate at which water percolates down from the surface to subsoil levels (*see* page 13).

Cleaning the Ground

The need to plant shrubs on weed-free land cannot be stressed too strongly, especially when planting ground cover shrubs. Chemical weedkillers should not, however, be applied indiscriminately. Their main use should perhaps be reserved for ridding dirty vacant land of weeds where either time for hand weeding and cultivations is limited, or it is impractical so to do – as for example on rocky ground. In these instances, planting must be delayed to allow harmful residues to disperse.

As already mentioned weeds should be forked out manually paying particular attention to those growing amongst the roots of nearby plants and hedges. After an initial clean up, hoe or cultivate the land as time permits – ideally every ten days during the growing season to kill seedling weeds and worry regrowth. Without doubt this is the best way to prepare for planting.

Weed Barriers

Where persistent weeds irritatingly encroach from adjoining land, consider putting up a weed barrier – provided there is not a mass of tree roots or other obstacles to contend with.

Along the boundary with weedy land, dig out a narrow trench (minimum depth 1ft((30cm)). Line the sides of the trench with rigid plastic sheet. Quickly backfill with soil to hold the sheets in place. A neater more permanent job can be made by concreting in, and in between, paving slabs placed on edge. However, the extra cost and time involved in installation is not always considered to be warranted.

Increasing Soil Depth

Where there is less than 1–1½ft(30–45cm) of topsoil, consider ways to increase the depth.

Topsoiling is one option. Simply spread a blanket covering of good topsoil evenly over the shrub bed or border when digging. When importing topsoil, be selective, and take care not to bring in trouble in the form of weeds, pests and diseases – or chemical contamination.

In extreme cases, it is sometimes necessary to bring in large quantities of topsoil to achieve the required 1–1½ft(30–45cm) depth. In so doing the level of the bed can be raised to unacceptable heights – say above the damp proof course or soaring steeply above paths and driveways. Here a change of tactic is required. One way round the problem is to excavate down to the required depth, keeping any good topsoil separate from the subsoil. Dig out a strip at a time and only work when soil conditions and weather are suitable. Return the excavated topsoil, plus imported topsoil to make up levels. To keep costs within bounds only attempt to excavate and topsoil on a small scale in preparation for setting out low growing choice shrubs.

Raised Beds

The construction of raised beds opens up new territory from the standpoint of both display and practical considerations. Raised beds represent a useful ploy to give height in flat landscapes. They focus attention on specimen plants or groups. In a similar vein to 'crown' beds and 'highback' borders (*see* Fig 15) raised beds have advantages on low lying wet soils. In some gardens they may make it possible to topsoil without excavation. When carefully sited they can dispense with the need to ever walk on the soil which is of particular importance to those gardening on heavy clay soils. Finally for anyone intent on growing lime-haters in chalk and limestone districts, raised peat beds of lime-free mix provide one solution. Although they bring rhododendrons, azaleas, pieris and heathers into the realms of possibility this is not a project to be undertaken lightly – keep it to a small scale. To go against the natural limitations imposed by local soils represents work and cost. The same observations apply when

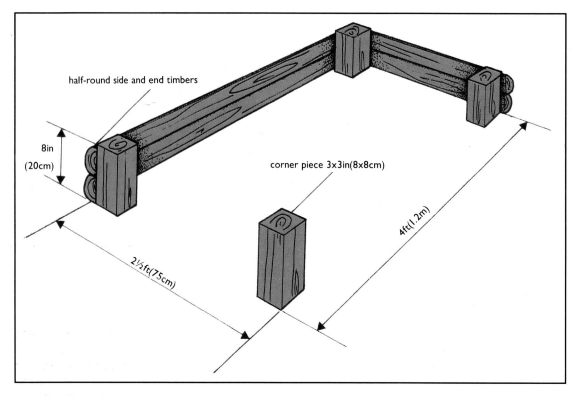

half-round side and end timbers

8in
(20cm)

corner piece 3x3in(8x8cm)

4ft(1.2m)

2½ft(75cm)

Fig 19 The raised bed. Bolt half-round timbers to corner pieces sunk
18in(45cm) deep. Fork up the base and fill with topsoil or prepared
planting mix. To make a peat bed, line the bottom with plastic sheet and
fill with lime-free peat-based mix.

other of the more temperamental shrubs are to be grown in what is to them an alien soil. Planting lime-loving clematis in an acid soil garden illustrates the point – make up a raised bed of suitable soil, or grow it in a container.

For details of construction of raised beds and peat beds *see* Fig 19.

Final Soil Preparations

Once levelling, draining and other preliminaries have been dealt with, a start can be made on final soil preparations, and these need to be thorough. Shrubs occupy the ground indefinitely and remedying deficiencies after planting is always more difficult and often wellnigh impossible.

The ideal is to double dig the entire planting area. This may not be in line with modern practice. But generally speaking, from the author's experience and observations, shrubs grown on deeply worked land are vastly superior to those set out after shallow digging.

Start by taking out a trench to a spade depth and width across the end of the bed. Fork up the bottom of the trench and work in peat, well-rotted garden compost or manure at the rate of at least one bucketful per sq yd(m). On heavy clay soils fork in coarse grit, sand or fine gravel at a similar rate to improve soil texture. Take out a second trench, throwing and inverting the topsoil into the first trench. Then fork up the bottom of the second trench – manuring and gritting as necessary. Continue thus, filling the last trench with topsoil from the first (*see* Fig 20). Prior to planting, rake in a handful of bonemeal per sq yd(m). Where the soil is suspected of being impoverished, work in some slow-acting base fertilizer in addition to the bonemeal. But never exceed manufacturers' recommendations.

26

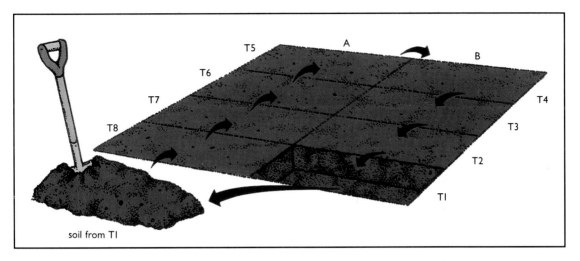

Fig 20 Double digging. Divide the bed into two halves A & B. Dig out a trench T1 10in(25cm) deep and place the soil beside T8. Fork up the bottom of T1. Repeat the process, filling T8 with soil from T1.

On heavy soils double digging is best carried out in autumn. This allows the soil to weather and break down under the alternate wetting, freezing and drying action of rain, frost, sun and wind. In spring when the soil is dry enough to work cultivate lightly, breaking down any remaining clods. Always work from planks to avoid overcompaction of the soil and prevent puddling.

Pocket planting is recommended when setting out single shrubs of all kinds as specimens, additions to the border or the odd replacement. It is also the best way of dealing with steep bank planting schemes. Planting pockets are prepared at planting time (see page 32).

Preparing for Hedging

In order to cope with the close planting and subsequent vigorous growth associated with hedging, extra attention to soil preparation is critical to success. In an average garden a single row of hedging is the norm. Prepare the ground along these lines:

1. Mark out the planting position of the hedge using a garden line and canes.
2. Hammer home pegs 1ft(30cm) each side of the line to mark out a 2ft(60cm) wide strip.

3. Dig out a 2ft(60cm) wide trench to a spade depth keeping the topsoil alongside.
4. Fork up the trench bottom, working in coarse sand or gravel if the soil is inclined to be heavy, as described for double digging (see page 26).
5. Bottom out the trench with a 2in(5cm) layer of well-rotted compost, manure or peat and scatter over a handful of bonemeal per yd(m) run of trench.
6. Backfill the trench with the topsoil.
7. Apply a layer of peat, manure or garden compost to the surface of the prepared trench at the rate of 1–2 bucketsful per yd(m) run. Lightly fork it in.

On average soils leave the surface practically flat. On low lying, wet or clay soils ridge up the central planting strip by about 3in(8cm). This is extremely important in high rainfall areas. At the other extreme, where the soil is light, sandy and quick draining, take out a central depression to trap rain and irrigation water, and plant in this.

Containers and Composts

Growing shrubs in containers offers plenty of potential, and the compost can be varied allowing a wider range of shrubs to be grown. Because

27

Fig 21 Hedges of mixed shrubs can be quite adventurous and should not be undertaken lightly. Here a mixture of purple and plain berberis is planted with honeysuckle.

containers provide a degree of mobility, tender plants can be moved under cover for the winter, further increasing shrub choice to include less hardy kinds. Mobility also makes rearrangement of displays possible so keeping up seasonal interest in prominent places. But perhaps the greatest scope containers have to offer is growing plants where it would otherwise be impossible, for example in courtyards and on balconies.

A well chosen container is an attraction in itself and will draw attention to the plants it houses. A good shrub container needs to meet certain basic requirements which are often confused and lost in the bewildering array of shapes, sizes and materials. These are:

1. Good looks.   Containers should be pleasing in design and appearance.
2. Strength and durability.   They should be strong enough to withstand frost and occasional knocks, be long lasting and weather and rot resistant.
3. Adequate size.   They should be deep and wide enough to prevent undue drying out and contain sufficient compost for root anchorage and to act as a reservoir of nutrients. The actual size will depend on the ultimate height and spread of the shrub. For a single bushy spreading shrub a minimum depth of one quarter shrub height and a minimum width equal to a third its spread gives a rough but reliable guide.
4. Good insulation.   Roots are vulnerable in containers. Good insulation gives protection against extremes of heat and cold.
5. Sensible shape.   For ease of repotting, watering and topdressing container sides should be vertical or taper only slightly —

narrowing towards the base. Avoid top heavy containers. If they are to be wind-firm they must be wider than they are tall.

6. Drainage holes. Holes in the base are essential to prevent waterlogging.
7. Weight. Watch the weight from a handling point of view. Lightweight plastic containers depend on weight of the compost for stability.

Most materials used in the manufacture of containers have their pros and cons:

1. *Wood* looks good, has excellent insulation properties but needs occasional treatment to prevent rotting.
2. *Concrete and simulated stone* are strong and durable and well insulated, but they are inclined to be heavy. Simulated stone and top of the range concrete can be highly attractive.
3. *Terracotta* allows for considerable flexibility in design and gives warmth of colour. However, it is liable to staining and is not always reliably frost hardy nor knock proof. Insulation is only fair.
4. *Plastics* score on the ground of cost. They are lightweight and have low maintenance but lose out on insulation properties. The use of fibre liners does help.
5. *Glazed ceramics* can be highly ornamental and decorative. But their frost resistance and knockability are suspect, particularly at the cheaper end of the range. Good quality ceramics tend to be very expensive.
6. *Metal* is occasionally used in the manufacture of containers. They tend to be costly, and unless treated or used in conjunction with liners, can cause metal poisoning to plants.

Preparation of Containers

There are a few points to watch when using new containers.

Check that wooden containers are free from preservative fumes. If in any doubt leave outdoors to weather for a week or two.

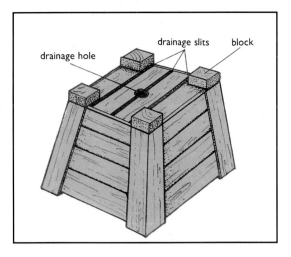

Fig 22   Containers need good drainage as well as legs or blocks to raise the base clear of the ground.

Soak concrete, simulated stone and terracotta in clean water overnight. This flushes out alkaline and other harmful salts. If containers are too large to submerge plug the drainage holes and fill with water. Subsequently unplug and drain.

Paint the insides of metal containers with rubberized bitumen paint. Allow to dry thoroughly before filling.

Old containers need meticulous cleaning before re-use. Brush off loose dirt, wash thoroughly using detergent, and disinfect with such as an approved tar oil derivative. Allow fumes time to disperse before filling.

Composts

Home mixed composts are the exception rather than the rule. Today the norm is to buy in ready mixed, pre-packed potting composts. They are reliable, save a lot of work and cost no more than home mixes.

Soil-based composts are better than peat-based mixes for shrub growing. Many peat-based mixes lose their texture after six to twelve months, and are more tricky to manage. Soil-based composts are well tried and tested. Use an average mix as a general purpose compost. A stronger mix is richer and well suited to very vigorous plants. General purpose, soil-based

29

composts are highly satisfactory too – provided the fertilizer content is adjusted. When dealing with lime-haters buy lime-free mixes.

Peat Bed Mix When growing lime hating shrubs in raised peat beds one mix which gives consistently good results is equal parts lime-free strong compost and sphagnum or moss peat. Mix thoroughly on a hard surface by spreading out a layer of strong compost and covering over with the peat. Turning the heap at least three times, using a spade, ensures an even distribution of peat throughout the compost.

Planting Mix Most bought in shrubs are growing in peat-based compost. When planted in the garden soil the roots have difficulty breaking out of the peat and into the soil. This is largely because peat and soil expand and contract at different rates on wetting and drying. To help overcome this problem 'planting mix' is used as backfill material. Sometimes these mixtures are referred to as transition soil. They contain more peat than garden soil and so make the transition easier, acting rather like a bridge. Proprietary soil-based composts work well – such as an average mix with or without lime as required. Alternatively if supplies of good topsoil are available use three parts loam topsoil to one part each of sphagnum peat and coarse sand. To every 8 gallons (= 3×2½ bucketsful) [36 litres] of mix add 8oz(220g) of bonemeal plus ¾oz(20g) of ground limestone. Omit the lime for limehaters. Mix as described for the peat bed mix but this time layering up soil, then peat, then lime, then sand and finally bonemeal on top. Store in a clean plastic bag if not required for immediate use.

Preparing the Plants

When dealing with well grown container shrubs, pre-planting preparation is minimal.

Little or no pruning should be needed, apart from shortening any straggly, damaged or broken shoots and roots back to sound wood and cutting out any dead, weak, inward growing, crossing or misplaced growths. However, do ensure that shrubs are well charged with moisture at planting time. Once planted it is often very difficult to re-wet a dried out rootball. Water containers at least twice, and allow an overnight rest between waterings and continue until water trickles out at the bottom. Submerge any dried out, neglected plants in clean water, with the water level just above the pot. Leave for twenty minutes or so. Then drain for half an hour before disturbing to plant.

Take extra care when planting any shrub, evergreen or deciduous, in full leaf during the adverse drying winds of late spring. Spraying the foliage with proprietary anti-wilt preparation is well worth consideration.

Planting Shrubs

Although container-grown shrubs can be planted out at most times of year, never attempt to plant when the ground is very wet, frozen, snow covered or bone dry and rock hard. Bear in mind early autumn or mid spring are the best times to plant evergreens, and autumn/early winter or spring in the case of deciduous kinds. Calm, mild, showery, dull weather is ideal for shrub planting. You should avoid setting shrubs out during hot, sunny, dry weather and when strong drying winds are blowing.

Some shrubs need to have a pollinator variety growing nearby if a good berry or fruit set is to be guaranteed. With most hollies, for example, male and female plants should be set out close together to ensure a good crop of berries. In hedging or group plantings one male to about four female plants should be about right.

Marking Out

Time spent measuring and marking planting positions is time well spent. In the case of permanent backbone shrubs – hedging and edging excluded – allow shrubs a minimum area equal to three-quarters their ultimate spread. When reckoning shrub 'spread' try to calculate a realistic size having due regard to climate, soil, treatment and time-scale. In cold gardens and on poor soils, for

Fig 23   On average soils (A), set plants at the same depth as surrounding soil. On heavy wet soils (B) plant on a slight mound, but on dry sandy soils (C) plant in a slight hollow to catch rain-water.

instance, the size of shrub is likely to be below the average stated on the label or in the catalogue. Hard clipped, formal shrubs can be contained in a much smaller space than free-form specimens which are allowed to grow virtually unchecked. Make allowances for this aspect, and when it comes to long lived, slow growing shrubs like camellias, there is merit in limiting the planting space to the likely size of the shrub in say ten years.

Do not overlook the nearness of shrubs to paths, driveways, foundations and windows. Aim to plant no nearer than a distance equal to three-quarters the ultimate height of the shrub. Other-wise the risk is root damage, and overhang in the case of drives, paths and windows. Keep climbers and wall shrubs at least 10in(25cm) out from any wall. This is not only for the good of the wall but will also avoid excessive drying out.

Planting in Prepared Beds and Borders

A planting hole of at least twice rootball diameter, and half as deep again as rootball depth, will normally suffice. Dig out and try for size by placing the shrub in the hole, complete with container. Adjust as necessary in keeping with the following recommendations. On aver-age soils the shrub should rest finally with the top of the rootball about 1in(3cm) below the surrounding soil level. Increase the depth slightly on quick draining, sandy soils in dry districts. Conversely, in areas of high rainfall on heavy soils allow for the rootball to be slightly raised.

Fork to loosen up the bottom of the hole, working in extra peat and a small handful of bonemeal. Bottom out with a few handfuls of planting mix. If the ground is very dry, water the hole and allow to drain before positioning the shrub in the centre. Remove the container carefully, tease out the roots at the base of the rootball, and spread them out trimming back any which are damaged. Backfill with planting mix, firming with the foot as filling proceeds. Level off taking particular care not to leave a depression around the base of the stems on heavy soils. On sandy soils, however, it is sound practice to dish the soil to trap rain and irrigation water.

Hedge Planting

In the case of hedges, ground preparations and planting often form part of one continuous operation to avoid double working. However, if the ground has been prepared well in advance of planting and the topsoil reinstated, start by taking out a narrow trench. Make it half as wide again as the average rootball width, and deep enough to comfortably take the roots when the top of the rootball is set about ¾in(2cm) deeper than the surrounding soil. A garden line pulled taut makes a useful guide, both when making the trench and when planting.

From here on treat the plants in much the same way as when planting in the border – watering the trench beforehand in dry weather, forking in peat and bonemeal and bottoming out with planting mix. Ensure that the final level of soil and plants is related to soil type and climate – raised slightly on a ridge on clay soils in wet areas, or sunk in dry districts on sandy soils.

Some authorities favour setting out hedging plants diagonally in the row – cordon fashion – arguing that this makes for thicker hedge bottoms. Based on long experience the author favours vertical planting. Growth is quicker and the problem of diagonal plants at row ends is avoided. Given good plants and a modicum of care, there should be no problem of lack of even branching at the base of vertical plants.

Pit or Pocket Planting

Specimen shrubs – and rock garden shrubs – are best planted in pits or pockets. In grassed areas the first step is to remove a sufficient area of turf to allow room for comfortable working, and stack it to one side.

Dig out a planting hole. For specimen shrubs a good average size is 1½ft(45cm) square and 1ft(30cm) deep. Always allow a 4in(10cm) clearance around the rootball. When dealing with shrubs in large containers, increase the hole size to at least double rootball width and half as deep again as container depth.

Fork up the bottom of the hole and loosen the sides. Bottom out with a 1½in(4cm) layer of peat plus a good handful of bonemeal and fork it in. On heavy soils work in some sand or grit at the same time. Mound up a few handfuls of planting mix in the centre of the hole and then complete the planting as for shrubs in borders.

In grassed areas replace the turf but leave a minimum 2ft(60cm) collar of bare earth around the base to reduce competition for food and moisture. Use any surplus good turves for patching the existing lawn.

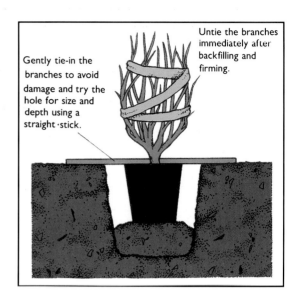

Fig 24 Pocket planting.

When pocket planting small shrubs in rock gardens, simply scale down the size of individual pockets. After planting top-over the soil with limestone chippings or such as a granite aggregate –always use acid or neutral aggregate for limehaters. Neglect to top-over and much of the soil may be washed away during winter. When

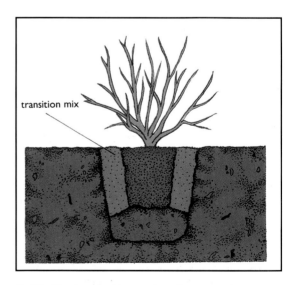

Fig 25 Shrubs raised in peat-based compost establish more quickly where a soil:peat:sand transition mix is used for backfilling instead of in situ soil.

space for bulbs and bedding plants

Fig 26   Plunging a shrub, complete with pot into a tub of potting compost enables bulbs and bedding plants to be set out without damage to shrub roots.

planting limehaters always be sure to use lime-free potting compost or planting mix.

Planting in Containers

When planting shrubs in containers, it is just as important to match shrub with site as when planting in any other part of the garden.

Having selected a container big enough for the job position it over a drip tray. Ideally allow for a minimum air space of 1in(3cm) beneath the container to assist drainage. Secure gauze or net over the drainage holes using very fine mesh materials. This should prevent soil pests gaining entry through the drainage holes. Cover the bottom of the container with a generous layer of crocking, clean gravel, small stones or pieces of polystyrene – again to assist drainage.

To plant a single shrub, part fill the container with potting compost – preferably soil-based. Use a lime-free mix for limehaters. Never be tempted to use ordinary garden soil. Not only is it likely to contain soil pests and diseases, but it is not fertile enough for container work. It is neither the right texture for satisfactory aeration and drainage nor is it likely to contain sufficient nutrients.

Having removed the shrub from its container, tease and spread out the roots and position the shrub so that the top of the rootball rests 1in(3cm) below the rim, to allow for watering. Work more compost around the roots and firm.

To plant a shrub grouping, gauze, crock and part fill the container as before. But this time either potting compost or peat can be used. The shrubs are then set in the container still in their original pots. However if these are of the floppy type or obviously too small, repot into rigid pots of an appropriate size, before plunging. Potting compost or peat is then packed around the pots up to their rims – again leaving space for watering and feeding.

33

CHAPTER 3

Routine Aftercare

IMMEDIATE AFTERCARE

Watering

Water all shrubs immediately after planting. This settles the soil around the roots and ensures an adequately moist root run. Dryness at the roots is especially dangerous for newly planted shrubs.

Proprietary preparations, which help to maintain soil moisture levels, are making their way onto the market, but are used mostly by contractors. They work on one of two principles. Firstly, there are those which act rather like a surface mulch. They stabilize the soil and reduce evaporation. Secondly there are granular products which absorb rain and irrigation water and

hold it against gravity, releasing moisture as the soil dries out. Although claimed to be environmentally friendly, treat these products with caution until more is known about them and experience is gained.

Shelter

In exposed gardens it is advisable to provide at least temporary protection from the damaging effects of buffeting by cold, freezing or drying winds. Evergreens are most at risk. Fine mesh netting, supported on a light framework will suffice for temporary shelter. Give protection on three sides, backing the screen into the prevailing wind.

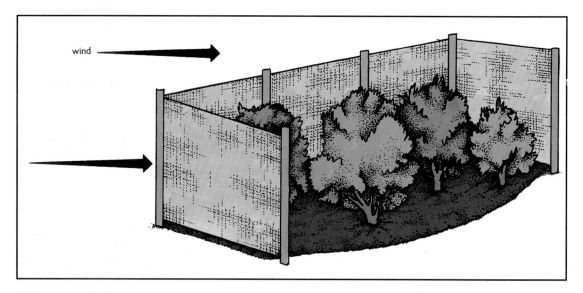

Fig 27 A temporary windscreen. Fine mesh netting on supports, backing the screen into the prevailing wind makes shelter for a group of shrubs.

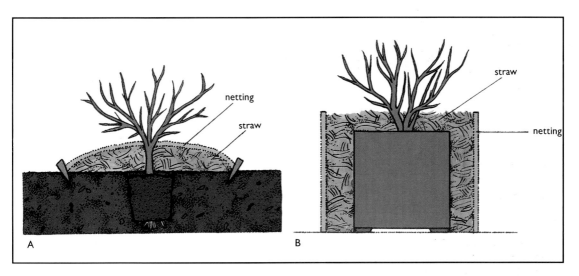

Fig 28   Frost protection. (A) A layer of straw held down with netting helps to protect frost sensitive roots of newly planted camellias and magnolias during their first winter. (B) Straw completely surrounding the roots of container shrubs and held in place with netting gives valuable frost protection during winter.

Root Protection

In cold climates, many hardy shrubs are liable to root injury during severe frost in the first winter or two after planting. Camellias and magnolias are representative of shrubs which are particularly sensitive in this respect. Putting down a thick 4–6in(10–15cm) wad of straw as a collar is one effective way to ensure a good measure of protection. Hold it in place with pegged down netting. And be sure to cover the entire root run. A 2in(5cm) layer of peat or bark chippings makes a reasonable alternative to straw.

Spraying

During their first spring and summer after planting, shrubs benefit from having their foliage syringed over in warm, dry or windy weather. Use clean water and spray in the evening.

Some shrubs, such as wisteria and magnolia, are slow to start growing the first season after planting, and daily syringing can help by breaking the dormancy and encouraging new growth.

Anti-wilt sprays – sometimes referred to as anti-desiccants – can be useful. They are of particular benefit to evergreens, and any other shrub planted when in full leaf, especially if set out into less than ideal situations. These foliage sprays help to reduce moisture loss caused by wind and sun.

ROUTINE CARE IN AUTUMN AND WINTER

A large part of the shrub scene during autumn and winter is taken up with protection against the elements.

Firming and Soiling

Guard against windrock movement and ground heave. Newly planted shrubs are very vulnerable in this respect. It is almost inevitable that shrubs which have not had time to become securely anchored are blown about. However, other shallow rooted mature kinds like crataegus,

35

escallonia and forsythia also suffer – no more so than when grown on heavy soils. They are loosened, and the surface roots may even be exposed to wind and sun. Following windrock movement of this sort, a space is likely to form at the base of the shrub – into which water collects to start the rotting process. Matters are made worse through ground movement and heave resulting from the action of frost.

Refirm the roots by treading. But wait until the thaws come, the weather is mild and the ground not overwet. Spread on sufficient potting compost to cover any exposed roots and infill any cavities around the base. Temporary shelter, as mentioned previously, goes a long way towards preventing excessive windrock in the early days. In notoriously exposed gardens, think in terms of providing permanent shelter – hedges, planting screens and landscape walling are all suitable.

Frost Protection – Roots

Mention has already been made of the need to protect the roots of some young shrubs and has already been discussed. Similar remarks apply to a number of established shrubs of borderline hardiness when grown in cold winter areas. For instance under these circumstances, hardy fuchsias, caryopteris and variegated hypericum all need protection. Straw, peat or shredded bark should be in place in autumn before the onset of damaging frosts, and there it should remain until all risk of hard frost has passed when it should be pulled aside from the root run to allow the soil to warm up.

Frost Protection – Tops

Frost damage occurs in a variety of ways. Very low temperatures can cause splitting of soft or tender growths, resulting in a progressive dying back and rotting. Frosting and blackening of leaves, flower buds and open flowers is a form of injury frequently associated with a rapid thaw. A fairly typical situation arises when shrubs are subjected to an overnight frost. Follow this with bright early morning sun, as is common to east-facing sites, and an overquick thaw is likely. The result is frost damage to flowers, leaves, shoots and branches.

Marginally hardy wall plants and climbers like abutilon, leptospermum and passiflora, along with any early flowering varieties and evergreens inadvertently planted on east-facing sites, are quite easy to protect. Drape fine mesh netting over the branches and attach it to the wall.

In all but the mildest areas, free-standing, winter flowering shrubs such as winter flowering viburnum, *Rhododendron praecox* and *Lonicera fragrantissima* (bush honeysuckle) benefit from the protection of fine hairnet-like mesh. This gives some wind as well as frost protection, at the same time allowing the flowers to be seen.

Selective Thinning

As the garden matures, selectively thin out temporary fillers, shrubs and herbaceous plants before overcrowding becomes a problem.

End-of-Season Clean Up

Take time during autumn or winter to clean up shrub beds and borders. The older the shrubs the more important this becomes.

Grub out any dead or dying shrubs. Gather up the remains of any prunings, rubbish, leaves and weeds. Lightly fork over the spaces between shrubs, working in any remains of organic mulches like peat or garden compost. But do not cultivate too deeply and take care not to damage roots. Be sure to relieve any compacted areas – if necessary work in coarse sand or gravel to open them up. Treatment of this nature is most likely to be needed around shrubs which are regularly cut for flower arranging. On heavy soils it is worth putting down a few stepping stones to provide for easy picking in all weathers and minimizing the risk of soil compaction. Deal with any wet spots or standing water promptly. As a first measure push a garden fork down vertically 6–10in(15–25cm) at intervals around the wet spot. Rock it to and fro once or twice. If the water drains away fairly quickly, scatter coarse sand or chippings over the fork holes to keep them open. In the event of water not getting away, more drastic measures like sump drainage may be required (*see* page 24). Apply lime where necessary. Once every three years would be average. Do not apply lime in the immediate vicinity of lime-haters (*see* chapter I).

Snow Shaking

After heavy snowfalls, gently shake shrubs to dislodge the snow. Evergreens are most likely to suffer broken and damaged branches simply because their foliage holds a greater weight of snow than the bare branches of deciduous kinds.

For pest and disease control *see* chapter 6, and for planting *see* chapter 2.

WINTER CARE OF CONTAINER SHRUBS

Safeguards against the Weather

Container shrubs have a lower frost resistance than comparable shrubs of the same variety which are planted direct. This is largely due to the fact that frost is able to penetrate the root-ball from the sides as well as the top. The result is much lower root temperatures. Take steps to protect container shrubs during autumn before the onset of damaging frosts.

Indoor protection is really only necessary for immature young plants and mature shrubs which are verging into the frost sensitive category. These include *Hebe speciosa* and some varieties of abutilon and fuchsia. A well ventilated greenhouse or cool conservatory provide excellent winter quarters.

When grown in containers most of the really hardy shrubs – those classed as HI – overwinter safely if moved up against a warm wall. Make them secure so that they do not roll about in high winds.

As an added precaution, give extra root protection to valued shrubs in the form of a straw jacket kept in place with netting (*see* Fig 28).

In districts of high rainfall, it is worth covering the top of container rootballs with plastic sheeting to prevent waterlogging. Make sure that the roots are thoroughly moist before covering. Thereafter check regularly – they must not be allowed to dry out.

Potting It is important to see to potting and repotting of deciduous shrubs in autumn. Annual potting is the norm in the case of young shrubs, and every two or three years for older more mature specimens.

ROUTINE CARE IN SPRING AND SUMMER

Spring Clean

When starting on a neglected garden, hand-weed and gather up the remains of weeds, rubbish and, most importantly, prunings.

Fork or lightly cultivate soils inclined to be heavy, as soon as the ground is dry enough to work. This is to relieve compaction and break up the surface crust while controlling new weed growth.

Hoe or lightly cultivate sandy, easy-to-work soils to kill weeds and create a dust mulch. This helps to reduce the loss of soil moisture on un-mulched ground.

Continued surface cultivations in the form of shallow forking, hoeing or light cultivations are ideally carried out at 7–10 day intervals during the height of the growing season. In early spring and towards the end of summer, weed growth is slower and less frequent working is necessary. Surface mulching is sound practice and where carried out, late spring and summer soil cultivations can be largely forgotten about.

Topdressing is most likely to be needed in the rock garden where shrubs have been set out in planting pockets. But topdressing is sound practice wherever there has been any appreciable wash out or settlement. Carefully draw any gravel chippings or other mulch to one side. Lightly loosen the soil before applying fresh potting compost as a topdressing to make good any losses. Replace and replenish the surface mulch.

Continue refirming and soiling over of exposed roots on newly planted shrubs as and when necessary.

Planting

Ideally set out shrubs during dull, showery weather in mid-spring. Delay the planting of any marginally hardy varieties until late spring (see chapter 2). When planting out in early spring, be sure to have frost cover materials to hand, especially in the case of the marginally hardy. Netting, plastic sheeting or even an upturned bucket for overnight protection of small shrubs can all help.

Wind Protection

In exposed gardens, give newly planted shrubs the benefit of temporary shelter from cold and drying spring winds, especially from the east (see page 34).

Mulching

The application of a surface mulch around shrubs – climbers and hedging plants included – is an invaluable aid to good management. It is possible to grow shrubs without mulching – reasonably well in fact in the cooler and moister areas. However, in the warmer and drier southern and south eastern regions, mulching has much to offer. Growth is improved and work cut to a minimum.

Mulching helps in several ways, firstly by reducing the rate of soil moisture loss through evaporation. By acting as a weed-smother not only is competition for available nutrients and moisture reduced, but the need to hoe and weed is virtually a thing of the past. Mulching also evens out the extremes of temperature, keeping roots cooler in summer. The physical protection

Fig 29 Good mulching practice: 1) Hoe off small weeds and loosen the surface soil; 2) Apply topdressing feed (if necessary); 3) Water in, making sure the soil is well moistened; and 4) Spread a layer of mulching material over the soil.

afforded by a mulch cover reduces soil compaction and surface crusting, and in turn assists water percolation. Finally, some mulches enrich the soil with nutrients as they rot down.

Give newly planted shrubs first priority for mulches for at least a couple of years after they are set out. Healthy, established shrubs are better able to fend for themselves.

Mulching is normally best carried out in spring – once the soil has started to dry out and has warmed up a bit. Never apply mulch to frozen, snow covered or very wet and cold soil. Traditional mulches act as insulators and maintain the prevailing conditions at the time the mulch goes down, for example, if a mulch is applied to cold ground the soil would be slow to warm up. If mulching is missed in spring, then summer mulching makes a good second best.

In the case of established shrubs, mulching would be carried out along the following lines. Hoe or cultivate the soil to loosen the surface crust, kill the weeds and aerate the top few inches of soil. Shrubs which need feeding are

A plastic collar helps smother weeds and conserve soil moisture where other mulching materials are scarce.

Fig 30 Mulching.

then dealt with. Apply a general complete fertilizer and rake it in (for rates *see* page 42). If the soil is dry, water thoroughly before applying the mulch. Any newly planted shrubs would only need watering — fertilizer having been incorporated in the planting mix. Bulky materials like bark, peat, garden compost and manure are spread on the surface of the soil so as to completely cover the root run of each shrub in a 2in(5cm) layer. Take care not to pile mulches up against, or in direct contact with, the stems or you will risk rotting. Gravel chippings are normally applied more thinly — to a depth of about 1in(3cm). For details of using and laying plastic mulch (*see* Fig 30).

Mulching Materials

The traditional mulches are garden compost, leaf mould and well-rotted farmyard manure. Nowadays the choice is somewhat extended with the arrival of plastics and various forms of bark. Below is a list of some of the better known and more readily obtainable materials in everyday use for mulching.

1. Bark chips are attractive to look at. They are slow to rot and rob the soil of nitrogen in the process, thus shrubs may suffer unless extra feed is given. They may also contain weed seed, and pest and disease organisms and can often attract wood lice. They are fairly costly.
2. Bark composted looks similar to peat. Good samples are weed, pest and disease free. It contains some nitrogen and may attract ants and wood lice. It is moderately expensive.
3. Farmyard and stable manure is variable in quality. Good samples are reasonably rich in plant nutrients and brown and crumbly when well-rotted. It may contain weed seed, pest and disease organisms. Avoid samples containing wood shavings, sawdust or medicaments. Cost is variable.
4. Garden compost is cheap to make but the quality is variable. Poorly made compost may contain weed seed but should be nutrient-rich when well made. It should be brown and crumbly with a slight earthy smell.
5. Grass clippings if short make useful additions to the compost heap. However, they should be mixed with coarse materials, otherwise they may form an airless, porridge-like poultice.
6. Leafmould is cheap if composted at home. Oak and beech leaves are among the best leaves to use. Well-made leafmould is dark brown and flaky, but can contain weed seeds and disease organisms. Uncomposted leaves are not recommended for mulching. They

39

rob the soil of nitrogen and are slow to rot down.

7. Mushroom compost is best when composted with garden waste. Some samples contain relatively high percentages of lime. Play safe and do not use mushroom compost on limehaters.

8. Peat, either sphagnum or moss is brown, fibrous and acid and ideal for limehaters. It is tricky to re-wet if allowed to dry out and is fairly costly. Sedge peat is dark brown and near to neutral, and often cheaper than moss peat. However some samples can be dusty and others greasy and these should be avoided. For practical purposes peat has no nutritional value.

9. Black plastic sheeting used as a mulch helps to conserve soil moisture but tends to attract sun, heat and slugs. Thin grades break down within about two years. Once secured with stones or pegs at the edges it makes a relatively inexpensive mulch cover. The appearance is greatly improved if topped over with a covering of chippings or bark – a practice which also helps to overcome the tendency of plastic to attract sun heat.

10. Stone chippings are quite attractive, but moderately costly. They are used mainly to top over planting pockets in rock gardens and for topping off container shrubs. Use limestone chippings for the majority of shrubs but acid granite chippings for limehaters.

Watering

Incorrect watering, too much or too little, is one of the main causes of failure amongst shrubs, especially those grown in containers.

If plants are to grow properly an adequate supply of moisture is essential. Lack of moisture retards many of the essential life-giving functions. Wilting of the leaves and dry soil or dry potting compost are obvious outward signs of water shortage. When leaves wilt the ability of plants to manufacture starches and sugars is greatly reduced and these are needed for cell building within the plant. It is not always realized that once plants have wilted they cannot restart manufacturing starches and sugars immediately they are recharged with water. There is anything up to a 72 hour delay. Evaporation of moisture from leaves helps to keep a plant cool in strong sun – cool enough in many instances to allow the manufacture of food to continue in hot weather, otherwise it grinds to a halt. Efficient evaporation, however, can only take place from turgid, unwilted leaves.

Plants can only absorb and utilize nutrients when dissolved in solution. Lack of moisture slows down the upward movement of nutrients and moisture from the roots. Similarly, starches and sugars manufactured in the leaves cannot be moved around the plant and down to the roots except in solution.

Finally, low levels of moisture inhibit a plant's ability to breathe and grow.

Mention should also be made of the fact that most shrubs are capable of taking in water through their leaves as well as their roots.

The need to water established shrubs is most likely to arise during dry spells between late March and October. At this time more moisture is taken up by plants – and lost from the soil in drainage and surface evaporation – than is made up by natural rainfall. Shrubs most at risk, and therefore needing priority for watering are those newly set out, spring planted shrubs along with anything growing within a confined root space such as in raised beds or containers.

Ideally water shrubs in the cool of the day when the sun is not actually shining on the foliage – no matter whether early morning, late afternoon or evening. Strong sun playing on wet foliage is likely to result in scorch, because of the magnifying-glass effect of water droplets. If the wetting of leaves in strong sun is unavoidable then take immediate steps to shade the plants.

When to water often raises doubts. Clear-cut cases of water being needed are immediately before and immediately after planting, as well as

Fig 31   A moisture meter can determine if watering is necessary.

shrubs which are obviously dry and on the point of wilting. But as a routine, never wait until shrubs start to wilt before watering. This is too late for safety especially with leathery leaved kinds like azaleas, camellias and magnolias. Another fairly clear-cut case for watering is before mulching in spring.

Problems of when and how much water to apply also arise in less clear-cut cases. One way round the immediate problem, until experience is gained, is to use a moisture meter and there are various types to choose from.

For containers a very simple, low cost solution is to use water signals. These vaguely resemble plant labels and are pushed into the potting compost in close proximity to the roots — one per shrub with the top half exposed. The signals change colour depending on the moisture content.

For direct planted shrubs, more sophisticated battery operated moisture meters are suitable.

Popular makes have probes which are pushed into the soil. The moisture level is indicated by a flashing light or a direct read-off dial.

After a little while most gardeners can judge instinctively when water is required by looking at and touching soil, potting composts and leaves.

Having established that water is needed, apply at least 2 gallons per sq yd (10 litres per sq m) over the root run in beds and borders for newly planted shrubs in their first season. When watering established shrubs, comfortably double the rate. Never apply water in dribbles. This is bad practice which encourages surface rooting and does more harm than good.

Container shrubs are watered from the top, continuing until water trickles out at the bottom. But do check that the water is not simply running down between rootball and container side. Incidentally, if the compost has shrunk back appreciably it makes good sense to infill the gap with moist potting compost. Be prepared to water container shrubs at least twice a day during the height of summer.

When dealing with the small scale watering of an average garden a watering can with rose is adequate for most of the time. It is much more difficult to judge quantities accurately with a hose pipe. If a hose is used, be sure to use a rose attachment. Otherwise the jet of water will wash away valuable topsoil from around the roots where it is most needed. Sprinklers such as the oscillating type, provide a gentle curtain of irrigation water. They tend to be wasteful, but are of particular value on heavy soils which are less likely to become compacted by sprinkler application.

In dry districts, water penetration can be assisted by dishing the soil — making a depression around the base of each shrub to hold irrigation and rain water. This is not a practice for heavy soils.

There is need for caution in the matter of water quality. In hard water districts, for instance, the mains supply contains considerable amounts of lime which is detrimental to limehaters. Wherever possible in these situations, collect

Draw up soil to form a low circular ridge, making a dish, to aid watering in hot and dry conditions preventing run-off. Level off the ridge in autumn.

Fig 32   Dished soil.

and use rainwater. Avoid using water which has passed through a domestic water softener, as in some cases this may be even more harmful than using hard tap water.

Spraying

During dry weather most shrubs will benefit from syringing over the foliage with clean water during the evening, especially after particularly warm or windy days.

Feeding

In this environmentally or 'green' conscious age, the feeding of plants with man-made artificial fertilizers is increasingly being called into question. But in spite of all the talk, the fact still remains that plants do need a balanced diet of nutrients. Another of the facts of life is that soils are depleted of these life-giving nutrients in a variety of ways – they are washed out in drainage water, they are used up by plants and by soil organisms.

Manures and fertilizers can safely be used to replenish nutrient reserves in the soil in sufficient quantities to sustain reasonable plant growth. What needs to be avoided is the build up of excess nutrients like nitrogen in the soil which endangers water supplies and life. Another equally dangerous side effect of the misuse of fertilizers is the build up of harmful waste residues in the soil. Correct liming helps to neutralize these residues, and it also renders nutrients more readily available to plants. Provided environmentally friendly plant feeds are used wisely, applied in the right amounts at the right time and in the right way, no harm need arise.

Shrubs need nitrogen, phosphorus and potassium for healthy growth (NP&K) plus various trace elements. Among these iron, magnesium, manganese and boron are the most important.

Nitrogen is necessary for leaf and shoot growth. Too little results in poor growth but excess results in too much growth at the expense of flowers and fruits. Phosphorus is needed for good root development and early maturity. Deficiency and excess both result in stunted growth. Potassium imparts hardiness, disease resistance and quality, and improves the general well being of the shrub.

Trace elements are essential to general good health and performance of shrubs. Iron and magnesium for example help to ensure the smooth production of starches and sugars.

Fertilizers are concentrated sources of nutrients. They come in various forms prepared from minerals and/or organic matter (plant and animal remains). By and large organic-based fertilizers are safer to plants and the environment than inorganic or mineral-based ones.

When applying fertilizers of any kind always follow the manufacturers' instructions closely. At the present time most gardeners could get by comfortably using bonemeal (organic) together with a complete organic-based fertilizer containing N P & K, plus trace elements. Bonemeal, which supplies phosphorus and nitrogen is used mainly as a pre-planting slow-acting fertilizer.

Complete fertilizers are used in various ways, depending on the maker's formula. Dry complete fertilizers are used as pre-planting fertilizers, in potting composts and in planting mixtures.

They are applied between late winter and early summer as a post-planting topdressing to both direct planted and container shrubs before mulching. A small handful per sq yd (m) spread over the root run would be an average dressing but read the label carefully and follow instructions closely. In the case of container shrubs this is an alternative to topdressing with potting compost.

Avoid applying fertilizer in late summer or autumn or you will risk soft, frost-prone growth which is unable to stand up to the rigours of winter.

Soluble complete fertilizers make useful root drenches. When dealing with direct planted shrubs, they are applied in weak solutions during spring and summer when a boost is needed. Apply at 21–28 day intervals if growth is moderate or poor, and stop for a time if growth becomes excessive. In the case of container shrubs liquid feed as a matter of routine. An average timetable would be feeding once a month during summer. But, as with direct planted shrubs, stop if growth becomes excessive. When liquid feeding container plants, water normally, allow to drain for a couple of hours, and then root drench with liquid feed continuing until it starts to trickle out at the bottom. On occasions, soluble fertilizers are applied as foliage feeds, but only use grades intended for the purpose, and then view them purely as a quick-acting tonic to correct nutrient deficiencies, or as a stop-gap where the roots are damaged and unable to function properly.

Apply all liquid feeds during dull weather, and ensure the roots are moist prior to application.

Foliar feeds are the quickest to take effect –

usually in 1–7 days. Liquid root drenches take 7–10 days. Dry topdressings take longer to act and allow 14–21 days. Much depends on the time of year and temperature, watering, the site conditions and upon the plant itself.

The term manure loosely refers to bulky organics. They are used for mulching in spring and summer. They are dug into the soil during planting preparations. Some, like farmyard manure and garden compost, release nutrients – including valuable trace elements, and all improve soil texture.

For pruning and training *see* Chapter 4, for propagation *see* Chapter 5 and for pest and disease control *see* Chapter 6.

SPRING AND SUMMER CONTAINER CARE

In spring, when all danger of frost has passed, move containers from their winter quarters and clean them up.

See to the potting of evergreen shrubs. Move young shrubs into larger containers and re-pot established mature kinds into the same container. Topdress where potting is not called for – established shrubs are usually only repotted once every two or three years. Remove the top 1in(3cm) of old potting compost. Replace it with fresh compost, using lime-free mixtures where appropriate. Do not forget to topdress those deciduous shrubs which were not re-potted in autumn. Topdress too any other shrubs where the compost has been washed away during winter. Start the spring and summer routine of watering and feeding.

CHAPTER 4

Pruning, Training and Grooming

WHY PRUNE?

An understanding of why shrubs are pruned should help to clear up some of the doubts and apprehension with which the job is all too often approached. You should prune:

1. To develop or maintain a pleasing shape.
2. To aid health, vigour and well being.
3. To regulate the flowering and fruiting wood. This helps to ensure that over production is avoided and quality maintained.
4. To channel a plant's energies into sustaining a long, useful and productive life.

Always prune with a definite purpose in mind and never cut shrubs about indiscriminately.

Pruning and Vigour

The effect of pruning a healthy shrub is to stimulate activity and promote growth. As a general rule, hard pruning results in vigorous growth, whilst a light cut back encourages growth of a less vigorous nature. Relate this knowledge to the previous chapters and it should become obvious that pruning intensity must be linked closely to feeding, watering and rainfall.

Generous feeding, hard pruning and a plentiful supply of moisture usually results in vigorous growth, delayed maturity — and fewer flowers and fruits. You may, however confidently expect these to be of improved size and quality.

Light pruning, minimal feeding and dry conditions are conducive to restricted growth, early maturity and prolific flowering and fruiting. However, blooms and fruits are normally of a smaller size and, in the case of flowers, carried over a shorter period.

Timing of Pruning

The timing of pruning can be critical.

Deciduous shrubs are ideally pruned immediately after flowering or fruiting. This allows the maximum interval before flowering comes round again. The shrub then has adequate time to make new wood and build up reserves of energy. It is best to avoid pruning in late winter. Once the sap has started to rise, there is a risk of bleeding (excessive loss of sap). This weakens the shrub and it can all too easily become disease prone. Unless the aim is to restrict growth, avoid heavy pruning in summer. Autumn pruning promotes vigour.

Evergreens too are best pruned after flowering or fruiting. In this instance though, try to restrict pruning to the warmer months of the year — between May and September. Otherwise risk winter frost damage. Never prune any shrub during severe or prolonged frost. The risk is stem splitting, disease entry and possible dying back.

The Basics of Pruning

The age, condition and habit of the shrub in question all have a bearing on how it should be pruned. As indeed do the aims and objectives of the moment. For example where formal effects and a geometric outline are the aim, then frequent and regular cutting or clipping are called for. Selective thinning, on the other hand, creates a less rigid appearance.

Pruning Cuts

All cuts should be made cleanly without any suggestion of chewed, ragged or torn edges which are unlikely to heal quickly. Open wounds of this nature are vulnerable to disease attack and very often the consequence is subsequent rotting.

Ensure that all pruning tools from knives and pruners to saws and shears are clean and sharp while for ease of handling, all moving parts should be well lubricated. Use pruners for cuts up to ¾in(2cm), and a pruning saw for cuts over ¾in(2cm). These larger cuts should be smoothed over with a sharp knife and promptly painted with a proprietary sealant.

When shortening a damaged or spent stem to sound wood, either cut it back to just above (⅛in(3mm)) a healthy bud or flush with a main branch. Angle the cut slightly so as to shed water away from the bud (see Fig 34). Neglect to do this and water lodging in the vicinity of the bud is likely to start rot. Never leave snags (small stumps without buds or side growths). Without the stimulation of buds or side shoots snags can only rot off, and ultimately they will die back.

Fig 33   Paint over all pruning cuts of ¾in(2cm) and over with proprietary sealant to keep out wet and prevent entry of disease organisms.

Pinching is widely used in the training and shaping of standard and bush forms. Take a sharp knife or pruners to remove the tips (growing points) of stems and shoots. This encourages branching and thickening up lower down.

Clipping is used extensively in the shaping of hedges as well as in the creation of topiary shapes and geometric effects. Cut back all new growths, more or less uniformly, to within ½in(1cm) of older wood. A close knit, densely-textured mat of shoots and foliage should result.

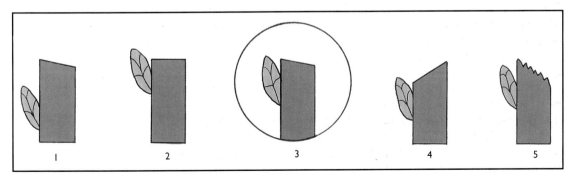

Fig 34   The basic pruning cut. Cut cleanly just above a sound bud as in 3. The cut is too high in 1, too close in 2, slopes the wrong way in 4, and is jagged and disease-prone in 5.

Fig 35 When cutting off branches of any appreciable size, always undercut quarter way through before cutting down from above. This reduces the risk of branch splitting.

Thinning is largely used to maintain the health of bushy shrubs. Cut out growths selectively in order to let in more light and air. The result is a freer, more open-textured, natural shrub.

Heading back or crown reduction is used to considerably reduce the height and width of a shrub. A fairly drastic cutting back of the branches is involved, (see Fig 38).

Pruning Young Shrubs

When dealing with young shrubs, pruning and training go hand in hand. Pruning should start early in the life of a shrub. Otherwise energy is wasted producing unwanted growths which are only removed at a later date. Also the sooner the initial training is completed, the quicker the shrub will settle down and contribute a useful display — be it foliage, flowers or fruits.

As already mentioned, any damaged or broken shoots should be cut back to a good bud on sound wood at planting time, with weak or spindly shoots shortened back to a good stem or branch. In the event of damaged roots, cut back to sound healthy tissue.

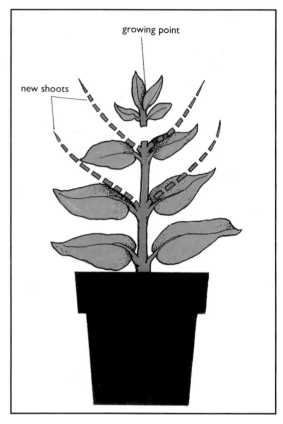

Fig 36 Pinching or stopping. Remove the growing point to make plants bushy.

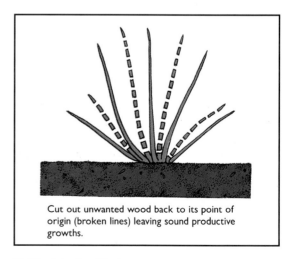

Cut out unwanted wood back to its point of origin (broken lines) leaving sound productive growths.

Fig 37 Selective thinning.

46

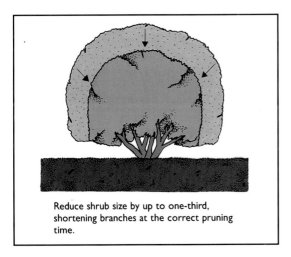

Reduce shrub size by up to one-third, shortening branches at the correct pruning time.

Fig 38   Heading back.

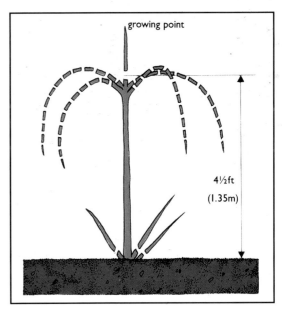

growing point

4½ft
(1.35m)

Fig 39   Training a standard Buddleia alternifolia. *Train up and support a single main stem, cutting out any others at soil level. Cut out the growing point and allow four shoots to grow to form the basic crown. Remove other growths lower down.*

Supporting and Tying

It is not necessary as a rule to support and tie average sized nursery stock. The exceptions are some wall plants and climbers. One of the best ways to deal with these is to tie them into trellis fixed to the wall, (*see* page 19), with the shoots spread out as evenly as possible over the area. In the case of fencing, tie in shrubs and climbers to straining wires. Large, extra heavy shrubs – as well as standards – should, however, be staked and tied. This is vital in exposed gardens.

Shaping Young Shrubs

1. *Bush forms*   Cut out weak and straggly shoots as well as those which are crossing and inward pointing. The aim is to keep bush forms open-centred to avoid overcrowding.

2. *Climbers and wall shrubs*   Allow climbers to cover their allotted space and then clip the grow-ing points to prevent further spread. In the case of wall and fence-trained climbers, aim to keep the top half of the rods horizontal. This en-courages even, free flowering.

3. *Standards*   One of the most popular forms of plant sculptures found in the garden. Many shrubs lend themselves to this form of training. It takes time and patience, plus a certain amount of know-how to train standards. However, the technique is within the grasp of almost anyone

---

The training of Buddleia alternifolia as a standard

Start with a vigorous, young, container-grown shrub. Remove all but one stem, selecting the strongest. Tie this in vertically to a stake at about 6in(15cm) intervals. Use proprietary ties so as to leave space for the stem to expand without strangulation. Thereafter, cut out any resulting side growths until the required length of clear stem has formed. Where say a standard with a 4ft(1.2m) length of clear stem is required, allow the main stem to reach about 4½ft(1.35m) – only then remove the growing point. Having removed the growing point allow three or four strong lateral shoots to develop, removing the weakest. When these laterals have made between 8in and 12in(20–30cm) of growth remove the tips. They will then form the main framework of the crown. At this stage, normal routine pruning can start – treating the 'crown' of the standard as a 'bush' shrub. During the training period make sure the shrub is kept well fed and watered so minimizing any setback to steady growth.

---

who is prepared to devote time and attention to detail provided 'easy' shrubs are tackled. The training of some – brooms, euonymus, azaleas

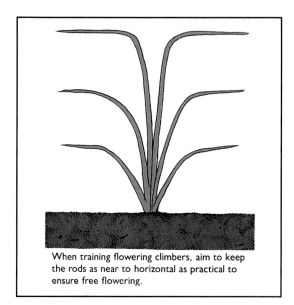

When training flowering climbers, aim to keep the rods as near to horizontal as practical to ensure free flowering.

Fig 40   Training climbers.

and rhododendrons included – involve budding and grafting techniques which are best left to the more experienced. This is no reason though why ready-trained forms of the more tricky kinds should not be bought in. They are relatively easy to manage once the initial training is completed. Anyone contemplating exhibiting standards should study the relevant rules for exhibitors before the completion of training.

4. *Simple espaliers*   For those who are unfamiliar with espaliers, they are wall trained shrubs with characteristic pairs of outstretched branches, arranged in tiers, fishbone fashion.

5. *Simple fans*   Various climbers, including ivies and *Clematis montana* as well as wall trained shrubs like *Chaenomeles speciosa* (flowering quince) and *Jasminum nudiflorum* (winter jasmine) are eminently suitable for fan training. Starting near ground level, train the branches out fanwise onto supporting trellis or wires. Remove the growing point of each branch once it has put on sufficient growth. If there are less than six to eight branches low down, remove the growing points from the strongest. This encourages branching and you should tie in the resulting laterals as they grow.

6. *Simple topiary*   Small leaved evergreens such as *Buxus* (box) and *Lonicera nitida* (evergreen honeysuckle) are among the most suitable shrubs for topiary work. Success depends on forming a basic framework of branches. Where curved shapes are the aim, tie in the main stems when young and supple to a pre-formed wire frame. Once the initial framework has been created, regular and frequent clipping is required.

7. *Hedges*   By following a few simple rules it is a relatively easy matter to create and maintain an even textured, formal clipped hedge.

(a)   Aim to make and keep the top of the hedge slightly narrower than the base. Otherwise you risk bare stems and gaps low down due to excessive shade and lack of light.

(b)   Clip small leaved shrubs, but use pruners on large leaved varieties to avoid untidy, ragged and discoloured foliage.

(c)   Cut newly planted deciduous hedges back by half to two thirds during the first dormant season after planting. Cut back slower growing broad leaved evergreens slightly less hard immediately after planting. Do not remove the growing points from conifers until the hedge has reached its required height.

(d)   After the initial cutting back, leave deciduous and broad leaved evergreen hedges a full year before further cutting to allow plants to become established.

(e)   Do not let a hedge reach its required height too quickly. Shorten back soft new

When clipping a hedge, keep the top narrower than the base to avoid bare stems.

Fig 41 Hedge training.

shoots by half their length, each time they put on 6–8in(15–20cm) of growth. Trim in the sides at the same time.

(f)   Once the required height is reached, clip regularly, each time taking new growths back to within ½in(1cm) of older wood.

(g)   With flowering and berrying hedges it is important to time hedge cutting so as to minimize loss of colour.

Where less rigid effects are required, occasional thinning and clipping are the norm. Always have due regard for the natural habit of the shrub. Do not, for example, cut off potential flowering wood unless completely unavoidable. Rhodo-dendrons illustrate this point well – if cut back a year's bloom is forfeited. Be ever mindful that informal hedges take up an enormous amount of space in a small modern garden.

Routine Pruning

Start by cutting out dead, damaged and badly diseased wood – right back to sound, healthy tissue. Remove weak, crossing and badly placed shoots, and shorten straggly growths. Thin out overcrowded, touching stems and branches, always removing the weakest first.

Cut out unwanted suckers on budded or grafted shrubs. These are shoots which arise at or near ground level. The resultant growth is inferior to the chosen variety and if suckers are left they weaken the shrub. In extreme cases they can take over with a smothering effect. In the case of some standards, suckers may arise up the stems and these should also be removed.

Remove reverted green shoots whenever they occur on variegated shrubs. Failure can result in disappointment as the green shoots take over from the weaker variegated ones.

Aim to dead-head young shrubs in their first few seasons as the flowers fade in order to reduce the strain on the plant.

Specific Pruning

In order to maintain a succession of new wood to replace worn out and redundant growth, the practice commonly referred to as renewal pruning is adopted. Luckily most shrubs fall into definite categories according to their needs.

Renewal Pruning Group 1 (PG1)

Spring flowering shrubs which carry their flowers on young wood produced the previous year.
Treatment   As soon as flowering is over, cut out spent flowered shoots back to within one or two buds of their point of origin. If necessary, thin out new shoots as well, removing the weakest first.

Renewal Pruning Group 2 (PG2)

Spring and summer flowering shrubs which bloom on both new season's wood and on wood formed during the previous year.
Treatment   As soon as flowering is over for the season, selectively thin. Start by removing the previous season's flowered wood. Then cut back weak or spindly new shoots.

Renewal Pruning Group 3 (PG3)

Shrubs which flower from midsummer to autumn at the tips of new season's wood.

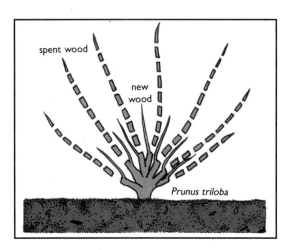

Fig 42 PGI In spring, as blooms fade, cut out spent flowering wood formed in the previous year. Train and tie-in replacement new wood for next year's display.

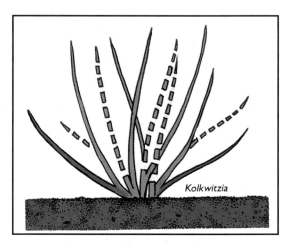

Fig 43 PG2 Remove about one quarter of the branches, starting with the oldest wood. Cut back weak growths to within two buds of their base.

Treatment In late autumn, shorten back spent flowering wood to within two buds of the point of origin. With some shrubs it is possible to prolong the flowering season. *Buddleia davidii* and late flowering spiraea are two good examples. They form main flower spikes which, if the tips are removed as the flowers fade, produce a second crop of smaller spikelets.

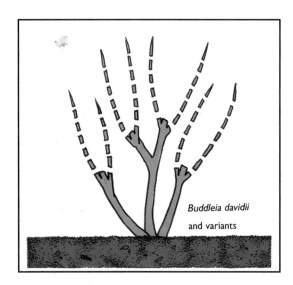

Fig 44 PG3 In autumn or late winter cut back the flowered wood to within two buds of the main framework.

50

Renewal Pruning Group 4 (PG4)

Shrubs grown for the winter beauty of their young bark.
Treatment Shorten back new wood to within one or two buds of the base in late winter or early spring.

Renewal Pruning Group 5 (PG5)

Naturally neat shrubs which require little or no pruning.
Treatment Shorten back the odd straggly shoot.

Renewal Pruning Group 6 (PG6)

Shrubs which stand clipping – or cutting back with pruners in the case of large leaved kinds.
Treatment Deal with evergreens in late spring or late summer. Deciduous kinds can be clipped from summer through to early winter.

Renewal Pruning Group 7 (PG7)

Mainly climbers and wall shrubs which need minimal pruning apart from confining to their allotted space.
Treatment Clip annually to restrict. Cut evergreens in late spring or late summer, and deciduous kinds during summer and autumn.

CHAPTER 5

Propagation

Shrub propagation can be a money saving, pleasurable and satisfying occupation, and, with a few notable exceptions, it is not all that difficult.

Those with valued shrubs could consider home propagation to raise replacements before the plant succumbs to old age. In the case of unusual shrubs, not readily available through normal outlets, this may be the only practical way to perpetuate such plants. When growing marginally hardy shrubs it makes good sense to use home propagation as an insurance against loss during a prolonged spell of severe weather. Take the odd cutting annually so as to have replacement plants to hand should the worst happen. Where any appreciable number of plants are required as for hedging, screening or ground cover the most economical way to tackle the job is to propagate. In this instance, buy in a few shrubs and use them as stock plants.

Before embarking on home propagation, consider the possible drawbacks. With some shrubs there may be an unacceptably long waiting period between starting off new plants and their reaching planting out size. Magnolias and camellias for example are notoriously slow growers. A few of the more tricky shrub varieties involve budding and grafting which are never easy for the inexperienced. With this in mind, think hard before attempting to propagate the likes of lilac, wisteria and standard brooms.

GETTING EQUIPPED

Where the aim is to raise only a few shrubs, using easy methods, it is possible to get by with a minimum of equipment.

1. A sharp knife and pair of pruners.
2. An assortment of pots, potting compost and coarse sand.
3. A few labels and some clear plastic bags.
4. A propagating frame – a deep wooden box with a sheet of glass or clear rigid plastic to cover the top will suffice.
5. A small heated propagator is a great help when dealing with some of the more fussy cuttings which root more quickly with a bit of bottom heat (see individual plant entries).

Obviously, a greenhouse or conservatory, plus a garden frame and automatic watering system may make life easier, but need not be classed as essential. In purely financial terms it is difficult to justify buying a greenhouse just for the sake of raising a few shrubs!

Raising Shrubs from Seed

Pre-Sowing Treatment

If seeds are to germinate, grow and flourish they need proper care from the moment they are harvested. If maximum vitality is to be preserved they should be stored in cool, dry conditions at about 41°F(5°C), or slightly less, until required for sowing.

Most hardy shrub seeds must have a period of wetting and chilling before they are able to germinate. Pre-soak medium sized and large seeds in clean water for six to eight hours at room temperature of around 60–65°F(16–18°C). Small seeds rely on wetting after sowing. During autumn and winter the seeds can be sown without further ado since they will receive the requisite period of chilling – quite naturally. In spring, when a natural chilling would be unlikely, an artificial method is called for. Mix the soaked seeds with damp peat and place in a clear plastic bag. Chill for twenty-one days in a domestic refrigerator prior to sowing. Sow small seeds and encase the entire container in a plastic bag – then chill in the refrigerator as before.

Sowing to pricking out

Small, clean pots are the most suitable containers for seed sowing, provided they have plenty of drainage holes in the base. Fill with fresh soil-based seed compost, lightly firming and levelling to within ½in(1cm) of the rim. Scatter the pre-soaked seeds thinly on the surface and barely cover with moist seed compost. In the case of pre-chilled seeds, scatter the seed/peat mix on the surface. Small seeds are sown thinly and gently pressed into the surface but are not covered with compost.

Water all seeds immediately after sowing by standing the containers up to half their depth in clean water. Drain after about twenty minutes, and cover the top of each container with clean plastic sheet.

Place the containers of unchilled seeds in a safe, vermin-free, shaded spot outdoors with the protection of a frame or a covered wooden box and then leave the seeds outside to chill for four to six weeks.

Germinate both naturally and artificially chilled seeds in warmth – at 60–65°F(16–18°C), shaded from direct light. When the seedlings are large enough to handle, prick them out – one to a small pot, using fresh soil-based potting compost. Germination can be erratic and it is often necessary to prick out the odd few seedlings over a period of time. Stand the pricked out seedlings in well lit positions under cover where a temperature of around 55–60°F(13–16°C) can be maintained.

Protect the tender young plants from strong sun. Again, be sure to use lime-free mixtures for lime haters.

Hardening Off and Growing On

Once the young plants are growing away freely, they should be gradually hardened off by increasing the ventilation. When they are suitably acclimatized, move them outdoors at the first opportunity during late spring or summer. Give them a sheltered spot, shaded from midday sun and then grow the young shrubs on outdoors for two or three years, keeping them fed and watered and potting on into larger containers as required. By this time they should be ready to plant out into their permanent positions. Give frost protection each winter during this period – a covered frame is ideal.

Suckers

Some shrubs increase naturally by means of suckers and offshoots which are growths arising at or below soil level. Autumn is a good time to remove rooted suckers as growth ceases for the season. Spring, just as growth recommences, makes a good second alternative for some shrubs.

Where suckers are sufficiently large and strong they can be replanted immediately in their permanent positions. In the case of smaller, less well developed suckers, potting up and growing on for a year or two works well.

Extreme care is needed when selecting shrubs from which to remove suckers. Suckers from grafted or budded shrubs are not suitable. Be guided by individual plant entries.

A few shrubs of clump or thicket-forming habit can be increased by carefully pulling away the soil and cutting out a well-rooted segment. Replant the segment in a suitable spot and water well. Make good the topsoil from where the segment was removed and likewise firm and water in.

Layering

Layering, in its many forms, is a particularly useful method of propagation for the amateur gardener. Much of its appeal lies in the fact that no special equipment is needed. It is also easy to execute with expectation of 100 per cent success rate – even with fickle varieties and including those which do not root readily from cuttings.

There are two possible textbook drawbacks to layering. First is the time it takes to form a self-supporting root system which can be up to two years. And second is the fact that only the odd layer or two can normally be pinned down from a single shrub at any one time.

The time factor is really only of consequence where a move is envisaged and unrooted layers have to be left behind. Otherwise there is little difference compared to cuttings. If anything the advantage of growth rate lies with layering – although the rooting process may be slow, layers continue to grow and develop apace. The results are good sized plants by the time they are self supporting on their own roots. The question of 'numbers raised' is not a problem either in the average garden situation where only one or two replacement shrubs are required.

The following methods of layering have been selected as being the best suited to the shrubs listed in chapter 7.

Conventional Layering

Although the traditional time to conventional layer is during autumn or spring, many broad leaved evergreens can be dealt with at any time between spring and autumn.

As a general rule, layering is normally reserved for climbers and basal branching bushy shrubs. This is simply because it is easier to layer young wood within easy reach of the ground.

1. Select a young branch of up to two or three years old within easy reach of the ground.
2. Remove any remaining leaves from a short stretch of stem some 8–10in(20–25cm) back from the tip.
3. Scoop out a shallow hole in the soil beneath the treated branch. Make it about 2in(5cm) deep and positioned so that when the stem is bent the bare length rests in the hole.
4. Carefully remove a 2in(5cm) long, thin sliver of bark on the underside of the bare stem at a leaf joint. Then kink (bend) the stem at that point. Some authorities advise cutting the stem slantwise half way through, but this is

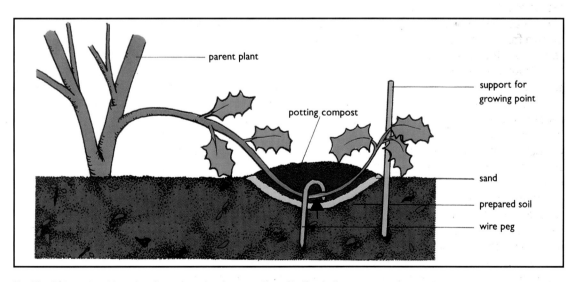

Fig 45 *Conventional layering. Remove a few leaves, plus a 2in(5cm) sliver of bark on the underside (arrowed). Peg down about 2in(5cm) deep on a bed of sand and cover with potting compost.*

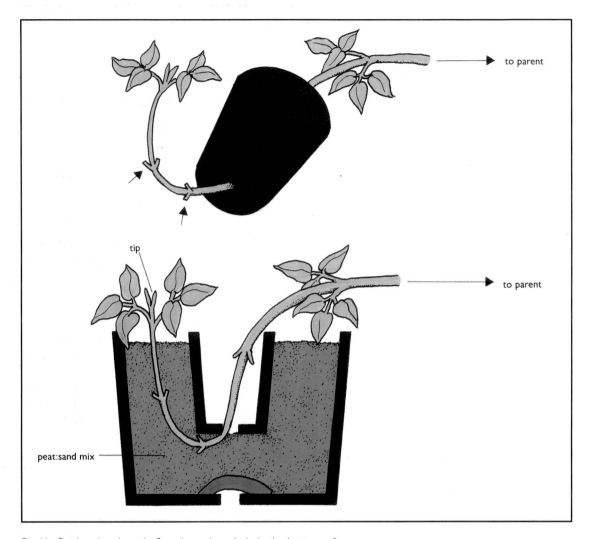

to parent

tip

peat:sand mix

Fig 46 Pot layering clematis. Step I – enlarge hole in the bottom of a small plastic pot. Remove 2 or 3 pairs of leaves (arrowed) and gently feed tip of the layer shoot out through the bottom. Step 2 – crock and part-fill a large pot with moist 50:50 peat:sand mix. Place pot and shoot inside the large pot and fill the intervening space with more peat:sand mix. Keep moist.

more risky, as it is easy to go too deep. Either method gives consistently good results.

5. Scatter sand into the prepared hole and pin down the stem at the kink using a piece of bent wire or a wooden peg.
6. Cover over the stem with potting compost – sufficient to level off the hole.
7. Keep watered and weed-free.
8. Once the tip has made any appreciable growth, stake and tie to an upright cane.

When well rooted and growing freely, usually in six to twenty-four months time, depending on variety, sever the stem which connects the young plant to the parent. But do not be too hasty to lift and transplant into its permanent position – delay a couple of weeks at least keeping it well watered in the interim.

In situations where it is not practical to layer direct into the ground, then improvise by layering into a container of potting compost.

Serpentine Layering

This is a variation on conventional layering and is worth consideration when propagating a quantity of plants from climbers like honeysuckle.

The procedure is similar to conventional layering except that each of the trailing stems is pegged down in several places – at alternate or every third leaf joint.

Once they are rooted and growing away nicely, sever the stem between parent and progeny as well as between each new plantlet.

Pot Layering

This is a technique which was developed primarily for propagating clematis but can also be used on other climbers like jasmine. Pot layering is normally carried out during summer, and the rooted layers are usually ready for planting out within nine to twelve months. Pot layering is perhaps best explained by means of illustrations, (see Fig 46).

Cuttings

The majority of the shrubs listed in chapter 8 can be propagated from either cuttings or layers. But it should be stressed that cuttings in general, compared to layers, are much more vulnerable to unfavourable conditions and neglect during the first few weeks of their existence. However cuttings do enable vast quantities of new plants to be raised from a single shrub – should the need arise.

There are a great many ways to prepare cuttings. here are some of the best and most successful methods.

Hardwood Cuttings

These are normally taken during the autumn or early winter. They are prepared from ripe, healthy wood of the current season's growth. Start off with longish shoots of about 1–1½ft(40–45cm) in length. Then using a pair of sharp pruners, cut off the bottom of each

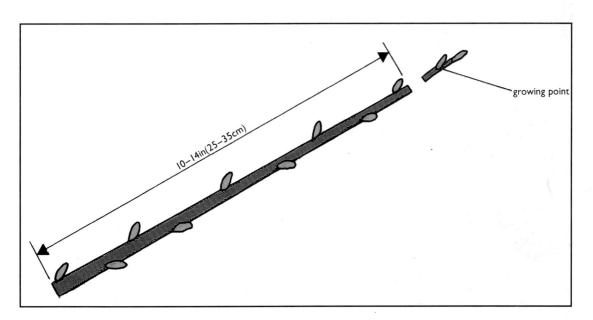

10–14in(25–35cm)

growing point

Fig 47   Preparation of a hardwood cutting. Cut clean below a bud at the bottom end of a pencil-thick shoot. Remove the soft growing point, cutting above a bud.

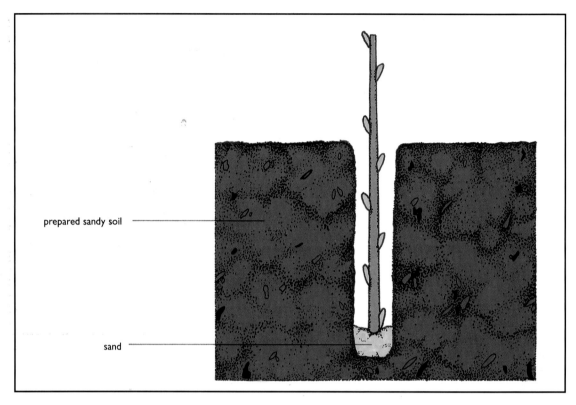

Fig 48   Rooting a hardwood cutting outdoors. Make a hole and trickle some coarse sand into the bottom. Insert the cutting to about two-thirds its length, resting the base firmly in the sand. Firm the soil around the cutting.

cutting, cleanly and squarely just below a leaf scar or joint. Similarly remove the tip ⅛in(3mm) above a bud – angled backwards and slightly downwards – *see* Fig 47. Aim for a finished length of prepared cutting between 10–14in (24–35cm).

In mild winter areas hardwood cuttings will normally root satisfactorily in the open, provided they are set out in warm, sheltered positions. This assumes of course that the soil does not lie cold or waterlogged. A sunny spot at the foot of a warm wall is excellent for the purpose. In colder winter areas some form of winter protection is recommended – a garden frame or cloches are ideal but be sure to remove any protective covering during mid to late spring.

Fork over a piece of ground, working in extra peat and sand and then tread to firm. Make a dibber hole for each cutting. These should be about 8in(20cm) deep and spaced about 6in (15cm) apart. Line the bottom of each hole with coarse sand. Insert the prepared cuttings, one per hole, so that the bottom of the cutting is in direct contact with the sand. Firm in, and water to settle the soil. Some authorities favour dipping the cuttings in a proprietary rooting preparation to hasten rooting but this is by no means necessary.

Keep the cuttings weed-free and well watered during the following spring and summer. In autumn, approximately a year after starting, quick growing shrubs can be planted out in their permanent positions. Slower growing kinds benefit from being left for at least another year before disturbing.

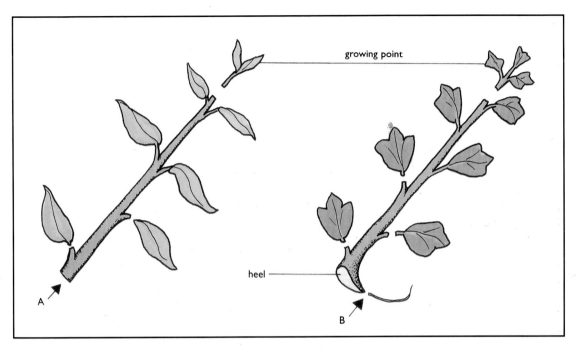

Fig 49 Semi-ripe cuttings. When preparing semi-ripe cuttings, remove the bottom 2-3 leaves, plus the growing point. Cut the lower end of a node cutting (A) just below a leaf joint. With a heel cutting (B) neaten off stringy bits of bark attached to the heel.

Semi-Ripe Cuttings (semi-hardwood)

These are usually started off sometime between early June and early September. It is the condition of the wood which is more important than the precise calendar date. But do leave time for rooting to take place before the onset of winter. Allow a minimum of eight weeks towards the end of the growing season. Aim to take semi-ripe cuttings as the wood is just starting to harden and become brittle. They are prepared from either healthy, vigorous side shoots or the tips of main stems.

Semi-ripe cuttings can either be cut off cleanly with a sharp knife or pulled away with a heel – a piece of old wood – attached. Either way they must always be taken at a time when fully charged with water. With this in mind take cuttings early in the day, or in the cool of the evening. If shrubs are dry, water thoroughly and leave overnight before taking the cuttings. Select 5–7in(13–18cm) long shoots which should neither be in flower nor carrying flower buds.

Trim those removed with a knife cleanly just below a leaf joint. Remove the bottom two or three leaves and cut off the soft tip just above a leaf, ending up with a prepared cutting of 4–6in(10–15cm) in length (*see* Fig 49). In the case of heel cuttings, shorten any straggly pieces of bark attached to the heel. Then as with the others, remove the lower leaves and soft tips.

The bottom of each cutting can be dipped in a rooting preparation though this is not essential. Insert the cuttings either singly in small pots of cutting compost, or place two or three around the edges. Make small holes with a pencil thick dibber and set each cutting just deep enough to hold it upright. Firm lightly then water in.

Root the cuttings in a greenhouse, garden

57

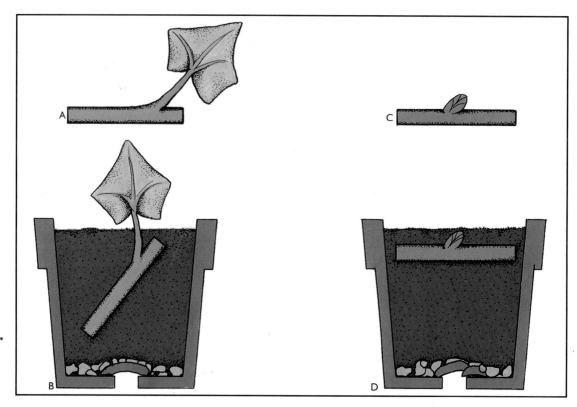

Fig 50   Leaf bud cutting (A): cut a 2in(5cm) semi-ripe stem section with a good bud and healthy leaf. Insert obliquely in a small pot filled with cutting compost (B). Eye cutting (C): cut a 2in(5cm) hardwood stem section (dormant) with a good bud. Insert horizontally about ¾in(2cm) deep in a pot of cutting compost (D).

frame or such as a wooden box with plastic or glass cover. In the absence of any of these alternatives, cover each pot with a perforated clear plastic bag and root on an indoor window sill. For the majority of shrubs, try not to let the temperature rise above 65°F(18°C). There are a few shrubs which do need some extra warmth and are best rooted in a heated propagator and you should be guided by individual plant entries.

Shade all rooting cuttings from strong sun and keep them moist by misting or syringing over the leaves daily with clean water.

When rooted, carefully pot up the young plants singly into small pots of potting compost.

Rooting usually takes place in anything from three to eight weeks, but much depends on the shrub variety and the degree of attention given to the cuttings.

Overwinter the rooted cuttings in such as a garden frame, and give extra frost protection during severe weather for the first and subsequent winters. Once all danger of frost has passed in spring, gradually increase the ventilation and place the young plants outdoors for the summer in a sheltered spot. Grow on for two or three years – potting on as necessary into successively larger containers. The young shrubs should then be ready to plant out in their permanent positions.

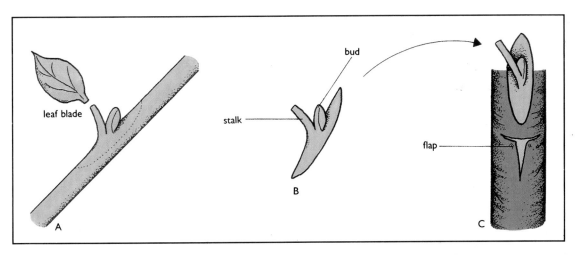

Fig 51 Budding. Select a good bud on the graftwood (A). Cut off the leaf blade, leaving a length of stalk attached to the bud. Cleanly remove a piece of bark, complete with bud, cutting along the broken line. (B) Side view of prepared bud. (C) Front view of bud ready to be pushed down behind the flaps of rootstock bark. When in position, bind with budding tape.

Leaf Bud Cuttings

These should be considered when propagating clematis, hedera and mahonia. There are a number of variations to this technique but all leaf bud cuttings are best taken during late summer using firm, semi-ripe wood of the current season's growth. Make sure the parent plant is well watered beforehand and prepare the cuttings starting with a 6–8in(15–20cm) length of shoot – slightly thinner than a pencil. Cut cleanly through the shoot in several places midway between each leaf, and insert the cuttings singly in small pots – or spaced out in trays – of cutting compost (see Fig 50).

Treat thereafter as semi-ripe cuttings.

Eye cuttings

One variation of leaf bud cuttings is eminently suitable for vitis – which can be increased using dormant buds or eyes. Eye cuttings are normally taken in early winter, immediately after leaf fall and before late December when the sap begins to rise. Vine eyes are placed horizontally, one per small pot and sunk about ½in(1cm) deep in cutting compost. Root in warmth at 65–70°F (18–21°C). Once growing away freely, treat as semi-ripe cuttings.

Budding and Grafting

Budding and grafting techniques are of a specialist nature. They ensure satisfactory growth, for varieties which do not grow satisfactorily on their own roots. This may be because they are not root firm, or are weak growing, or in the case of pendulous or weeping varieties do not produce strong stems of their own. In some instances budding and grafting can increase pest and disease resistance. Finally budding and grafting may succeed where other methods of propagation fail.

Budding and grafting are more usually left to commercial growers and nurserymen. Success depends on know-how, experience and skill and there is often difficulty in obtaining suitable rootstocks or understocks.

59

CHAPTER 6

Healthy Shrubs

As a rule, there is not the same degree of urgency or importance attached to pest and disease control among shrubs as to for example, edible fruits. In fact, pest and disease control amongst shrubs of all kinds is normally a very low key business, letting them take their chance without any special attention. This is not a sound policy to adopt as failures are disappointing and replacements expensive. Pests and diseases can and do spread to nearby gardens. Consider not only the negative but the positive and beneficial influences of healthy plants. A strong and healthy shrub almost invariably looks better and gives a superior and longer show of interest and colour than a sickly one.

AVOIDING TROUBLE

When it comes to combating pests, diseases and other shrub ailments, you should concentrate on prevention. It is much more likely to succeed than remedial treatment and, as a policy, is more in line with the present day trend to move away from the use of poisonous chemicals. For practical purposes, prevention entails adopting a code of good cultivation techniques. The aim is to grow a sturdy, vigorous shrub which will be much less likely to succumb to ailments than a weak, spindly one, and be much more likely to recover from a setback into the bargain.

PLAN OF CAMPAIGN

Essential points to watch in any programme designed to keep shrubs healthy are:

1. When planting, be sure to choose varieties which are well suited to the local climate, site and soil.
2. Avoid planting too many shrubs belonging to any one family — they are all subject to the same complaints.
3. Aim to set out healthy, pest and disease-free container-grown shrubs, and plant them in well prepared ground or in fresh soil-based potting compost.
4. Ensure that new and established shrubs have plenty of space, light and air. It is vital to avoid overcrowding with the resultant competition for daylight, moisture and nutrients. Give shrubs more than average space when growing in shaded borders.
5. Keep down weeds by cultivation and by mulching — again to cut down competition. Weeds also act as host, and provide hiding places and breeding grounds for pest and disease organisms.
6. Feed and water plants sufficiently to encourage steady growth and avoid starvation.
7. When pruning, use sharp pruners, saws and knives. Otherwise you risk leaving jagged or rough edges which are slow to heal and liable to disease infection and rotting.
8. Remove all litter, prunings and other debris promptly and as a matter of routine. They are likely to harbour pest and disease organisms. Ensure strict hygiene by adopting a regular routine of cleaning up operations in spring and again in autumn.
9. Cut out any diseased and seriously pest-infected wood and promptly dispose of the remains.

10. Keep a keen look out at all times for the first signs of trouble and act quickly to prevent pests and diseases getting out of hand.
11. Always wash hands and disinfect tools after dealing with diseased plants.
12. Hold chemical sprays in reserve until the outbreak of trouble. Never apply them indiscriminately.

THE IMPORTANCE OF DIAGNOSIS

It cannot be too highly stressed just how important is the need for correct and timely diagnosis. This is not always easy but it is an essential part of success. For instance, the application of fungicide when the problem is pest infestation is unlikely to do much good. Nor is there much future in applying insecticide if it is too late and the pests have already had their fill and departed.

PESTS

There are two main groups of insect pests which attack shrubs from time to time. First there are the chewing and biting kinds like caterpillars, weevils and grubs which feed on and hole leaves, buds and flowers. They are also responsible for chewed roots on occasions. The culprits are frequently to be found near the scene of their crimes. The other major group of pests which feed on shrubs do so by sucking the sap. Sap suckers usually congregate in colonies and are easily seen on leaves and stems, especially near growing points. Aphids and scale insects are typical sap suckers.

DISEASES

It is always tricky to identify diseases with any degree of accuracy. There are fungus diseases which, in their advanced stages, can often be identified by their mould and mildew outgrowths on stems, foliage, flowers, fruits or roots. Then there are the bacterial diseases which are notorious for causing wilts and rot of stems, roots, shoots and leaves. Lastly, there are the virus diseases which show themselves in leaf distortions and mottled and mosaic effects. Sometimes, though not always, wilting and death can follow. These three groups of diseases – fungal, bacterial and viral – are all infectious and are capable of rapid spread.

DISORDERS

It is inevitable that problems will manifest themselves if shrubs are subjected to poor growing conditions or an unfavourable environment. Fairly typical ailments to expect are leaf, bud and flower dropping, nutrient deficiencies and non-flowering. Disorders of this sort are not infectious.

Key	
Problem	Part Affected
P – Pest	L – Leaf
D – Disease	F – Bud, flower or fruit
DO – Disorder	B – Bark or stem
	R – Root

Aphid (various)   P/L and F

Symptoms

Puckering, distortion and curling of leaves, accompanied by colonies of greenish, bluish or black insects. These are to be found on leaf undersides, flowers, soft stems and particularly around the growing points. Aphids not only disfigure and weaken plants, but can also infect healthy shrubs with virus diseases after feeding on the sap of infected plants. Aphid attack nearly always results in honeydew – a shiny, sticky liquid in the vicinity of the colonies. In turn honeydew invariably proves to be an excellent medium for the growth of black, sooty moulds.

Treatment

Spray affected plants with insecticide and repeat as necessary during the growing season. Cut out heavily infected growing points and stems. Keep a special watch on euonymus, lonicera, viburnum and philadelphus which are all prone to attack.

Birds   P/F

Symptoms

The most serious form of bird damage is bud stripping. This occurs mainly during winter when the tell-tale leaf scales litter the ground beneath affected branches. In extreme cases, bare branches devoid of flowers and foliage result. Bullfinches are frequently to blame.

Treatment

Use bird proof netting over the likes of wall trained prunus and forsythia which are particularly at risk. Have it in position by October.

Bud and Flower Drop   DO/F

Symptoms

Buds and flowers drop at the slightest movement of branches. Often most noticeable in years of extra heavy flowering.

Treatment

Where over production of flowers is the fault you should regulate pruning. Refer also to entries on dryness and frost – camellias are very prone to bud dropping if subjected to dryness.

Canker (various)   D/B

Symptoms

Cankers develop on stems and branches. In the early stages they are generally seen as rounded or oval areas of brownish, greyish or blackish tissue. Each cankerous region is surrounded by raised rough bark. In the advanced stages, cankers can completely encircle branches and in such instances the branch tips, beyond the cankers, will die off.

Treatment

Avoid damage to bark when mowing or when pruning – canker gets a hold through open wounds. Always paint over large pruning cuts with proprietary sealant when pruning. Cut out cankers back to sound wood – chisel them out if necessary. Then pare off to smooth with a sharp knife prior to painting over with an anti-canker preparation.

Caterpillars (various)   P/L and F

Symptoms

Caterpillars are the immature stage of various moths, butterflies and beetles. They come in a variety of shapes, sizes and colours – greens, browns, oranges and striped. They may be smooth or hairy and are usually found near the scene of the damage they have caused. Expect holed and eaten leaves, buds, flowers and even fruits.

Treatment

Hand pick caterpillars to remove them where infestations are slight. Otherwise spray with insecticide and repeat as necessary at 14–21 day intervals throughout the growing season. Keep down weeds and ensure strict hygiene to eliminate any possible hiding places and to discourage further egg laying.

Following severe attacks, apply tar oil winter sprays to dormant deciduous shrubs in December – when they are leafless. Take care not to let the spray drift onto any evergreen shrubs or onto plants such as overwintering bedding plants.

Chlorosis DO/L

Symptoms

Typical of this nutritional disorder is stunted growth and the yellowing of leaves and growing points. Chlorosis is most likely to be a problem when lime-hating plants are grown in limy or chalky soils. Azaleas, rhododendrons and camellias are particularly sensitive.

Treatment

Don't plant lime-haters on chalky or lime-rich soils – grow them in containers of lime-free potting compost. Use rain water for watering in hard water districts. Give a root drench of iron sequestrene in spring or summer as the makers recommend.

Clematis Wilt DO and D (several factors may contribute to the cause)/L, F and B

Symptoms

Affected stems droop, leaves wilt and wither up. New shoots often break away from ground level – sometimes successfully, but more often than not only to wilt and wither up also. The problem is confined to members of the clematis tribe.

Treatment

There is no sure remedy. So, dig out and dispose of affected plants, complete with a large rootball of soil. Rest the ground for at least three years before replanting with clematis. Where there is some urgency to replant again, and no other climber will suffice, dig out a hole at least 1½ft(45cm) deep and 2ft(60cm) across. Disinfect the bottom and the sides of the hole with an approved tar oil derivative, taking care not to harm nearby plants. Allow fumes time to disperse before backfilling with clean soil-based potting compost or planting mixture.

Coral Spot D/B

Symptoms

Before attacking healthy wood the bright pink pustules first get a hold on dead wood – pruning snags being a common seat of infection. Most shrubs are liable to attack and the disease can be serious. Ribes and ligustrum are perhaps more at risk than most. *Nectria cinnabarina* is the fungus responsible and it spreads by spores from the pink pustules as well as by filamentous strands within affected plants.

Treatment

Never leave snags when pruning. Cut out and gather up all dead wood from around shrubs, including any lying on the ground. Cut out and dispose of any shoots bearing pink pustules. Practice strict hygiene and avoid overcrowding. When dealing with infected shrubs paint over *all* pruning cuts with sealant.

Damping Off (various) D/B

Symptoms

The stems of young seedlings become constricted at soil level before toppling over and dying off. If left, pink or whitish moulds will develop on the dead seedlings. Several different fungi can cause damping off.

Treatment

Prevention is the only satisfactory course of action. When sowing always start with fresh, clean compost and clean, disinfected containers. Adopt high standards of hygiene throughout. Sow seeds thinly and avoid overwatering. Where there is a history of trouble, putting a few crystals of potassium permanganate in the water can help (only enough to colour the water pink). Using seeds pre-treated with fungicide is a wise precaution.

63

Dieback (various) D and DO/B

Symptoms

Dieback may be due to one or more of several causes such as frost, wind, old age or incorrect pruning. It is usually seen as a progressive dying back of shoots and branches.

Treatment

Cut any dead growth back to sound wood, whenever noticed, painting over large wounds with sealant. Correct pruning faults. See entries for frost and wind.

Dryness DO/L and F

Symptoms

Bud, flower and fruit drop are commonplace — as is wilting, marginal leaf scorch and leaf drop. Growth becomes hard and stunted and in extreme cases death results. Problems of root dryness are made worse if drying winds and hot sun increase the rate of evaporation of moisture from the soil surface and from leaves.

Treatment

Attend to watering which is vital with container plants. With young plants, foliage spraying, mulching and shading from hot sun should be a high priority. Provide young plants with temporary shelter from wind — and in exposed gardens, see to permanent shelter. Check newly planted shrubs and cover over any exposed roots with potting compost and refirm after frost.

Fireblight D/L, F and B

Symptoms

Typically the leaves, flowers, shoots and even branches, of affected shrubs become blackened and withered as if burnt by fire.

Treatment

Cut off all affected parts, back to sound wood and promptly dispose of all prunings. Avoid planting susceptible shrubs like cotoneaster, pyracantha and stranvaesia in areas where fireblight is known to be a problem.

Frost DO/L and F

Symptoms

The blackening of leaves, buds and flowers after overnight frost and intense cold is almost too well-known to need description. Dead tips in a severe winter is a common occurence and many shrubs are affected.

Treatment

Prevention is the only satisfactory course of action. Give frost protection to young plants and to container-grown shrubs during the winter months. Grow marginally hardy shrubs on a warm, south or west-facing wall. Avoid planting evergreens — or winter and early spring flowering shrubs — on east-facing walls and fences. Otherwise you will risk a damaging over-quick thaw after overnight frosts because of the early morning sun common to these sites. Do not be too impatient to put indoor wintered shrubs outside in spring.

Honey Fungus D/L, F and B

Symptoms

Affected shrubs wilt progressively and ultimately die. Yellow, honey-coloured toadstools appearing at the base of diseased shrubs in late summer are the outward visible hallmark of honey fungus. The most usual means of spread is by underground bootlace-like strands which ramify through the soil to infect any woody plant within reach. Ligustrum is highly susceptible to honey fungus.

Treatment

Dig out and dispose of all infected shrubs and rhizomorphs (bootlaces). Drench the soil with a cresylic acid preparation between spring and autumn while there is some warmth in the soil. Allow fumes to disperse before replanting.

Mildews (various)   D/L and F

Symptoms

Leaves, buds, flowers and young shoots are all vulnerable to the white or whitish powdery coating common to this disease. Mildew not only disfigures but also stunts and distorts growth. Shrubs liable to infection include chaenomeles, clematis, cotoneaster, euonymus and hydrangea.

Treatment

Cut off any badly distorted and infected shoots on sight. Spray with fungicide at the first signs of attack and repeat at 21-day intervals during the growing season.

Mosaic   D/L and F

Symptoms

Typical effects of this virus disease include leaf mottling and yellow or whitish marbling of the foliage, combined with stunted growth. In the case of flowers, those affected show whitish streaks and colour breakings. Daphnes are particularly prone to infection.

Treatment

There is no cure and affected shrubs are a permanent source of infection. So, dig them up and dispose of them. After touching diseased shrubs, and before handling healthy ones, wash hands and disinfect knives and pruners in methylated spirits. Spray to control aphids which carry infected sap and spread the disease.

Non-Flowering   DO/F

Symptoms

Lack of flowers plus: Lush foliage and excess vigour. A mass of old worn out wood. Bare budless branches. Seemingly normal but unproductive growth. Frost and weather damage. Disease.

Treatment

1. Regulate excess vigour by correct pruning, restrained feeding and root pruning in extreme cases.
2. Avoid overcrowding when planting. Renew worn out wood by proper pruning and feeding.
3. For budless branches see entry on birds.
4. Normal but unproductive growth may be the consequence of inferior varieties. Accept the situation or replace with superior kinds.
5. Identify and combat diseases like fireblight.

Red Spider Mite   P/L and F

Symptoms

During severe attacks by this pest, the foliage becomes bronzed and mottled and growth is stunted. Fine webbing envelops the shoots and foliage with masses of minute red or yellowish red insect-like creatures on the leaf undersides. Attacks are worst in hot, dry weather. Wall shrubs and climbers are most at risk.

Treatment

Spraying the foliage with clean water during prolonged dry weather will discourage this pest — pay particular attention to leaf undersides. Where there is a history of attack, or at the first signs of trouble, spray with insecticide, and repeat at 14–21-day intervals during the growing season as the makers recommend. Keep a watchful eye on wall shrubs and climbers.

Reversion   DO/L and F

Symptoms

Reversion normally starts as a single plain green shoot on a variegated plant. If left the rogue shoot will take over and smother out the variegated foliage which, as a rule, is less vigorous.

Treatment

Cut out green shoots at source when they appear. Remove inferior suckers on sight.

Rusts (various)   D/L

Symptoms

In the early stages, rust is usually seen as yellowish-orange or rust-brown coloured pustules on the leaf undersides. In severe outbreaks whole leaves and stems are covered in rust coloured dust. Shrubs vulnerable to attack include berberis and mahonia.

Treatment

Cut out badly infected branches and apply a copper-based fungicidal spray such as Bordeaux mixture. Repeat as necessary.

Scab   D/L and F

Symptoms

In the main this desease attacks the berries — and sometimes the leaves — of pyracantha. Occasionally cotoneaster comes under attack as well. Expect the berries to be covered with a brownish or black coating.

Treatment

Where there is a history of scab, apply at least two fungicidal sprays in March or early April, allowing a 10-day interval between sprays. Repeat the two-spray programme in June.

Scale Insects (various)   P/L and B

Symptoms

There are many different kinds of scale insects but they all feed on leaves and stems by sap sucking. Look for clusters of grey, white or brownish blister-like bumps. Or in some instances, groups of small cotton wool-like tufts are more characteristic. Attacks are normally worst in warm and mild climates.

Treatment

Keep a watchful eye on likely victims like buxus, hedera, ilex, camellia, salix, syringa, cytisus and genista. Cut out badly affected shoots. On a small scale and on evergreens dab affected areas with cottonwool buds dipped in methylated spirits. In December, spray dormant deciduous shrubs with tar oil winter wash, as plant health regulations allow using maker's instructions. Be careful not to harm evergreens and other plants in leaf for example overwintering spring bedding plants. Scale insects are difficult to control.

Starvation   DO/L and F

Symptoms

Nutrient deficiencies manifest themselves in different ways, depending on which nutrient is in short supply. Suspect nitrogen deficiency if leaves are small and pale and perhaps yellowish, especially if accompanied by highly coloured fruits and stunted growth. Lack of potash is frequently seen as a purpling or browning and scorch at the leaf margins.

Treatment

Make sure that shrubs receive an occasional top-dressing of balanced fertilizer during late winter or spring. Preferably use an organic-based feed which contains essential trace elements like iron, magnesium, manganese and boron. Apply liquid feeds during the growing season if growth appears stunted and shrubs have not been potted or fed recently.

Waterlogging   DO/L and R

Symptoms

Where the subsoil drainage is at fault, waterlogging and drowning roots may not always be readily apparent. On the other hand, surface ponding and shrubs with water standing in collars formed by windrock, are soon spotted. Shrubs on heavy clay soils are most at risk and they are probably drowning or already dead if normally green leaves turn greyish and hang down and the roots smell of alcohol.

Treatment

Prevention is the only real answer. Drain and improve heavy soils before planting. When choosing shrubs for suspect soils go for moisture-loving kinds like cornus and viburnums. Avoid planting cytisus, genista and lavandula which have a preference for sandy, quick-draining soils.

Weevils (various)   P/L and R

Symptoms

When present in significant numbers various weevils can be highly damaging. They quickly devour semi-circular holes around the leaf margins of shrubs like azaleas, rhododendrons and vitis. There are other weevils which feed on the roots of these plants. The roots of parthenocissus and clematis are also at risk. Other weevils feed on the insides of flower buds of such as cotoneaster. The flowers fail to open and do not set berries. As weevils feed mainly at night – and hide during the day – they are not as a rule seen at work.

Treatment

Weevils are not easily controlled. Start by having a drastic clean up – removing all weeds, fallen leaves and rubbish from under shrubs and hedge bottoms. Leave no hiding places. Lightly cultivate the soil under affected shrubs, aiming to expose the weevils, and their immature grubs, to the view of garden birds which can consume vast quantities. When planting in the vicinity of shrubs likely to be attacked, avoid setting out the likes of primulas, which attract weevils.

Woolly Aphid   P/B

Symptoms

Signs of this pest are the very conspicuous patches of cotton wool-like covering on stems and bark. A close examination will reveal aphid-like insects under the cotton wool covering. Apart from looking unsightly, the woolly aphid feeds on plant sap and severely weakens and stunts plant growth. Cotoneaster and pyracantha are particularly susceptible to attack.

Treatment

Ruthlessly cut out and promptly dispose of as much of the affected wood as possible. Do this immediately it is seen. Paint over any remaining patches with methylated spirits, and repeat as necessary. Be wary about planting shrubs liable to infection anywhere near to apple, pear and thorn as these trees are also liable to attack.

Notes
1. See individual shrub entries for specific susceptibilities.
2. Always use approved chemicals and follow maker's instructions to the letter when using chemicals and proprietary preparations.
3. Never propagate from diseased shrubs. Nowhere is this more important than when dealing with viruses, as these are carried in the sap from one generation to the next.

CHAPTER 7

The Shrub Guide

NAMING SHRUBS

Plant names are a frequent source of irritation and frustration. Many newcomers, and for that matter many old hands too, shy away from using the latin technical names. Unfortunately, botanical names are a necessary evil in the correct identification of, trading in, and use of shrubs, and the reason is quite simple.

To avoid confusion botanical names — having been agreed by international convention — are accepted the world over by botanists, scientists and knowledgeable plant people alike. They will probably be used more rather than less, after the creation of a European community. Popular names often tend to be localized and can be a source of mistaken identity and disappointment.

Be careful and always order shrubs by their full name to be sure of getting what you want. Philadelphus illustrates this point well. *Philadelphus coronarius* has plain green leaves and grows to 10ft(3m) in width. Whereas *Philadelphus coronarius* 'Variegatus' not only has variegated foliage but makes a much smaller shrub altogether — growing only to 2½ft(75cm) in width.

You should be aware that from time to time the names of shrubs — and other plants — may be changed.

This is for a variety of reasons and is a state of affairs which creates considerable confusion for nurseries, garden centres and gardeners alike. Old established botanical names die hard, remaining in catalogues and gardening conversation for decades, long after botanists have decreed otherwise.

INDIVIDUAL PLANT ENTRIES

For the sake of convenience and to minimize confusion, current catalogue names are used in this section. The first entry is the botanical name and this is followed by the popular name.

Hardiness ratings are set out as follows: to summarise — plants rated H1 normally survive minimum winter temperatures of 5 to 10°F (−15 to −12°C). Corresponding figures for H2 rating are 10 to 20°F (−12 to −7°C) and for H3 rating are 20 to 30°F (−7 to −1°C). Pruning references refer to those explained on pages 49–50.

Care ratings are designated as easy, average or demanding according to the amount of attention needed by each shrub in an average garden situation.

The descriptions relate to the shrubs when grown under average outdoor conditions. Shrub sizes are approximate and average for mature free-standing specimens. Those grown in cold sites are likely to be below average in size. Expect those growing under ideal conditions in mild areas to grow well above the sizes stated. Similarly, wall trained varieties will be much larger too.

SHRUBS FOR SPECIAL PURPOSES

Selecting shrubs for special purposes can present something of a problem without some form of easy reference. In the following pages the 75 shrubs have been tabulated A–Z to enable the reader to find shrubs to meet the needs of the moment.

Table 1 – Shrubs for Seasonal Colour

Key
F - flower colour
Lv - coloured foliage
B - fruit or berry colour
AT - autumn foliage tints
S - stem or bark interest
E - evergreen year-round foliage

An example: when looking for shrubs with spring flower colour refer to the column titled 'spring' and read off the shrubs in the A–Z opposite F.

Table 1   Shrubs for Seasonal Colour

	Spring	Summer	Autumn	Winter	Year-round Interest
Abelia × grandiflora	–	F	F	–	E
Abutilon megapotamicum	–	F	F	–	–
Acer palmatum 'Dissectum Atropurpureum'	Lv	Lv	Lv	–	–
Actinidia kolomikta	Lv	LvF	Lv	–	–
Aesculus parviflora	–	F	AT	–	–
Artemisia 'Powis Castle'	Lv	Lv	Lv	–	–
Aucuba japonica 'Crotonifolia'	LvF	Lv	Lv	LvB	E
Berberis darwinii	LvF	LvB	Lv	Lv	E
Buddleia davidii 'Royal Red'	–	F	–	–	–
Buxus sempervirens	Lv	Lv	Lv	Lv	E
Callicarpa bodinieri 'Profusion'	–	F	AT	B	–
Camellia japonica 'Elegans'	LvF	Lv	Lv	Lv	E
Campsis radicans	–	–	F	–	–
Caryopteris × clandonensis	–	LvF	LvF	–	–
Ceanothus 'Topaz'	–	F	F	–	–
Chaenomeles × superba 'Knaphill Scarlet'	F	–	–	–	–
Chimonanthus 'Grandiflorus'	–	–	–	F	–
Choisya ternata	LvF	LvF	Lv	Lv	E
Cistus × corbariensis	Lv	LvF	Lv	Lv	E
Clematis 'Lasurstern'	–	F	F	–	–
Convolvulus cneorum	Lv	LvF	Lv	Lv	E
Cornus alba 'Sibirica'	S	–	–	S	–
Corylopsis pauciflora	F	–	–	–	–
Cotinus coggygria 'Royal Purple'	Lv	LvF	Lv	–	–
Cotoneaster conspicuus decorus	Lv	LvF	LvB	LvB	E
Cytisus 'Andreanus'	–	F	–	–	–
Danae racemosa	Lv	Lv	Lv	LvB	E
Daphne mezereum	F	–	B	–	–
Deutzia × 'Mont Rose'	–	F	–	–	–
Elaeagnus pungens 'Maculata'	Lv	Lv	Lv	Lv	E
Enkianthus campanulatus	F	–	AT	–	–
Escallonia 'Donard Brilliance'	Lv	LvF	Lv	Lv	E
Euonymus fortunei 'Emerald n Gold'	Lv	Lv	Lv	Lv	E
Forsythia 'Lynwood'	F	–	–	–	–
Fuchsia 'Riccartonii'	–	F	F	–	–
Garrya elliptica	Lv	Lv	Lv	LvF	E
Genista lydia	F	F	–	–	–
Halimium ocymoides	–	F	–	–	–

Table I Shrubs for Seasonal Colour

	Spring	Summer	Autumn	Winter	Year-round Interest
Hamamelis mollis	F	–	AT	F	–
Hebe × franciscana 'Blue Gem'	Lv	LvF	Lv	Lv	E
Hedera helix 'Goldheart'	Lv	Lv	Lv	Lv	E
Helianthemum 'Firedragon'	Lv	LvF	Lv	Lv	E
Hibiscus syriacus 'Woodbridge'	–	F	F	–	–
Hippophae rhamnoides	Lv	Lv	LvB	B	–
Hydrangea macrophylla 'Blue Wave'	–	F	F	–	–
Hypericum calycinum	Lv	LvF	LvF	Lv	E
Ilex aquifolium 'Madame Briot'	Lv	Lv	LvB	LvB	E
Jasminum nudiflorum	F	–	F	F	–
Kalmia latifolia	Lv	LvF	Lv	Lv	E
Kerria japonica 'Pleniflora'	F	–	–	–	–
Kolkwitzia amabilis 'Pink Cloud'	–	F	F	–	–
Lavandula 'Hidcote'	Lv	F	F	Lv	E
Leptospermum scoparium 'Red Damask'	Lv	LvF	LvF	Lv	E
Leucothoe fontanesiana 'Rainbow'	Lv	LvF	LvF	Lv	E
Leycesteria formosa	–	FB	B	–	–
Ligustrum ovalifolium 'Aureum'	Lv	Lv	Lv	Lv	E
Lonicera periclymenum 'Belgica'	F	F	–	–	–
Magnolia × soulangiana 'Lennei'	F	–	–	–	–
Mahonia aquifolium	LvF	LvB	Lv	Lv	E
Myrtus communis	Lv	LvF	LvB	Lv	E
Nandina domestica	Lv	LvF	LvB	Lv	E
Olearia haastii	Lv	LvF	Lv	Lv	E
Osmanthus delavayi	LvF	Lv	Lv	Lv	E
Pachysandra terminalis 'Variegata'	LvF	Lv	Lv	Lv	E
Parthenocissus henryana	–	Lv	AT	–	–
Passiflora caerulea	–	F	FB	–	–
Pernettya 'Mother of Pearl'	Lv	LvF	LvB	LvB	E
Perovskia × 'Blue Spire'	–	LvF	LvF	–	–
Philadelphus 'Belle Etoile'	–	F	–	–	–
Phormium 'Maori Maiden'	Lv	LvF	Lv	Lv	E
Photinia × fraseri 'Red Robin'	Lv	Lv	Lv	Lv	E
Physocarpus 'Dart's Gold'	Lv	LvF	Lv	–	–
Pieris 'Forest Flame'	LvF	Lv	Lv	Lv	E
Pittosporum tenuifolium	Lv	Lv	Lv	Lv	E
Potentilla fruticosa 'Jackman's Variety'	–	F	F	–	–
Prunus triloba	F	–	–	–	–
Pyracantha 'Orange Glow'	Lv	LvF	LvB	LvB	E
Rhododendron yakushimanum	LvF	Lv	Lv	Lv	E
Ribes sanguineum 'Pulborough Scarlet'	F	–	–	–	–
Robinia hispida 'Rosea'	F	F	–	–	–
Rosmarinus officinalis 'Miss Jessop's Variety'	LvF	LvF	Lv	Lv	E
Ruta graveolens 'Jackman's Blue'	Lv	Lv	Lv	–	–
Salix lanata	LvF	Lv	Lv	–	–
Salvia officinalis 'Purpurascens'	Lv	Lv	Lv	–	–
Sambucus racemosus 'Sutherland'	LvF	LvF	LvB	–	–
Santolina chamaecyparissus	Lv	LvF	Lv	Lv	E
Senecio 'Sunshine'	Lv	LvF	Lv	Lv	E
Skimmia japonica 'Rubella'	LvF	Lv	Lv	LvF	E
Spartium junceum	–	F	F	–	–
Spiraea × bumalda 'Anthony Waterer'	Lv	LvF	Lv	–	–
Stranvaesia davidiana	–	F	ATB	B	E

Table 1 Shrubs for Seasonal Colour

	Spring	Summer	Autumn	Winter	Year-round Interest
Symphoricarpos rivularis	–	F	B	B	–
Syringa velutina (syn *S. palibiniana*)	F	F	–	–	–
Tamarix pentandra 'Pink Cascade'	Lv	LvF	LvF	–	–
Viburnum tinus	LvFB	LvB	Lv	LvF	E
Vinca minor 'Variegata'	LvF	Lv	Lv	Lv	E
Vitis coignetiae	–	–	AT	–	–
Weigela florida 'Variegata'	Lv	LvF	Lv	–	–
Wisteria sinensis	F	–	–	–	–
Yucca filamentosa 'Bright Edge'	Lv	LvF	Lv	Lv	E

Table 2 – Shrubs for Special Features

From left to right the special features columns read: quick growing; dwarf or slow growing; medium to tall; scented; and arrangers (for cutting in moderation).

An example: a tick against a shrub in the first column – quick growing – indicates above average growth rate.

Table 2 Shrubs for Special Features

	Quick Growing	Dwarf or Slow Growing	Medium to Tall	Scented	Arrangers
Abelia × *grandiflora*	✓	–	✓	✓	✓
Abutilon megapotamicum	✓	–	✓	–	–
Acer palmatum 'Dissectum Atropurpureum'	–	✓	–	–	–
Actinidia kolomikta	✓	–	✓	–	–
Aesculus parviflora	–	–	✓	–	–
Artemisia 'Powis Castle'	✓	✓	–	✓	✓
Aucuba japonica 'Crotonifolia'	–	–	✓	✓	✓
Berberis darwinii	✓	–	✓	✓	✓
Buddleia davidii 'Royal Red'	✓	–	✓	✓	✓
Buxus sempervirens	–	–	✓	–	✓
Callicarpa bodinieri 'Profusion'	–	–	✓	–	✓
Camellia japonica 'Elegans'	–	–	✓	–	–
Campsis radicans	✓	–	✓	–	–
Caryopteris × *clandonensis*	✓	✓	–	✓	✓
Ceanothus 'Topaz'	–	–	✓	–	✓
Chaenomeles × *superba* 'Knaphill Scarlet'	✓	–	✓	–	✓
Chimonanthus 'Grandiflorus'	–	–	✓	✓	✓
Choisya ternata	✓	–	✓	✓	✓
Cistus × *corbariensis*	–	✓	–	✓	✓
Clematis 'Lasurstern'	✓	–	✓	–	–
Convolvulus cneorum	✓	✓	–	–	–
Cornus alba 'Sibirica'	✓	–	✓	–	✓
Corylopsis pauciflora	–	–	✓	✓	✓
Cotinus coggygria 'Royal Purple'	✓	–	✓	–	✓
Cotoneaster conspicuus decorus	✓	✓	–	✓	✓
Cytisus 'Andreanus'	✓	–	✓	✓	–
Danae racemosa	–	✓	–	–	✓

Table 2 Shrubs for Special Features

	Quick Growing	Dwarf or Slow Growing	Medium to Tall	Scented	Arrangers
Daphne mezereum	–	✓	–	✓	–
Deutzia × 'Mont Rose'	✓	–	✓	–	✓
Elaeagnus pungens 'Maculata'	✓	–	✓	–	✓
Enkianthus campanulatus	–	–	✓	–	✓
Escallonia 'Donard Brilliance'	✓	–	✓	–	✓
Euonymus fortunei 'Emerald n Gold'	✓	✓	–	–	✓
Forsythia 'Lynwood'	✓	–	✓	–	✓
Fuchsia 'Riccartonii'	✓	–	✓	–	✓
Garrya elliptica	–	–	✓	–	✓
Genista lydia	✓	✓	–	–	–
Halimium ocymoides	–	✓	–	✓	–
Hamamelis mollis	–	–	✓	✓	✓
Hebe × franciscana 'Blue Gem'	✓	✓	–	–	✓
Hedera helix 'Goldheart'	✓	–	✓	–	✓
Helianthemum 'Firedragon'	✓	✓	–	–	✓
Hibiscus syriacus 'Woodbridge'	–	–	✓	–	✓
Hippophae rhamnoides	✓	–	✓	–	✓
Hydrangea macrophylla 'Blue Wave'	✓	–	✓	–	✓
Hypericum calycinum	✓	✓	–	–	✓
Ilex aquifolium 'Madame Briot'	–	–	✓	–	✓
Jasminum nudiflorum	✓	–	✓	–	✓
Kalmia latifolia	–	–	✓	–	–
Kerria japonica 'Pleniflora'	✓	–	✓	–	✓
Kolkwitzia amabilis 'Pink Cloud'	–	–	✓	–	✓
Lavandula 'Hidcote'	✓	✓	–	✓	✓
Leptospermum scoparium 'Red Damask'	–	–	✓	–	✓
Leucothoe fontanesiana 'Rainbow'	–	–	✓	–	✓
Leycesteria formosa	✓	–	✓	–	✓
Ligustrum ovalifolium 'Aureum'	✓	–	✓	✓	✓
Lonicera periclymenum 'Belgica'	✓	–	✓	✓	✓
Magnolia × soulangiana 'Lennei'	–	–	✓	–	–
Mahonia aquifolium	✓	✓	–	✓	✓
Myrtus communis	–	–	✓	✓	✓
Nandina domestica	–	–	✓	–	✓
Olearia haastii	✓	–	✓	✓	✓
Osmanthus delavayi	–	–	✓	✓	✓
Pachysandra terminalis 'Variegata'	✓	✓	–	–	–
Parthenocissus henryana	✓	–	✓	–	✓
Passiflora caerulea	✓	–	✓	–	✓
Pernettya 'Mother of Pearl'	✓	✓	–	–	✓
Perovskia × 'Blue Spire'	✓	✓	–	✓	✓
Philadelphus 'Belle Etoile'	✓	–	✓	✓	✓
Phormium 'Maori Maiden'	–	✓	–	–	–
Photinia × fraseri 'Red Robin'	✓	–	✓	–	✓
Physocarpus 'Dart's Gold'	–	✓	–	–	–
Pieris 'Forest Flame'	–	–	✓	–	✓
Pittosporum tenuifolium	✓	–	✓	✓	✓
Potentilla fruticosa 'Jackman's Variety'	✓	✓	–	–	–
Prunus triloba	✓	–	✓	–	✓
Pyracantha 'Orange Glow'	✓	–	✓	✓	✓
Rhododendron yakushimanum	–	✓	–	–	–
Ribes sanguineum 'Pulborough Scarlet'	✓	–	✓	✓	✓

Table 2 Shrubs for Special Features					
	Quick Growing	Dwarf or Slow Growing	Medium to Tall	Scented	Arrangers
Robinia hispida 'Rosea'	✓	–	✓	–	✓
Rosmarinus officinalis 'Miss Jessop's Variety'	✓	–	✓	✓	✓
Ruta graveolens 'Jackman's Blue'	✓	✓	–	–	–
Salix lanata	–	✓	–	–	✓
Salvia officinalis 'Purpurascens'	✓	✓	–	✓	–
Sambucus racemosus 'Sutherland'	✓	–	✓	✓	✓
Santolina chamaecyparissus	✓	✓	–	–	✓
Senecio 'Sunshine'	✓	✓	–	–	✓
Skimmia japonica 'Rubella'	–	–	✓	✓	✓
Spartium junceum	✓	–	✓	–	✓
Spiraea × bumalda 'Anthony Waterer'	✓	✓	–	–	✓
Stranvaesia davidiana	✓	–	✓	✓	✓
Symphoricarpos rivularis	✓	–	✓	–	✓
Syringa velutina (syn S. palibiniana)	–	✓	–	✓	✓
Tamarix pentandra 'Pink Cascade'	✓	–	✓	✓	✓
Viburnum tinus	✓	–	✓	–	✓
Vinca minor 'Variegata'	✓	✓	–	–	✓
Vitis coignetiae	✓	–	✓	–	✓
Weigela florida 'Variegata'	✓	–	✓	–	✓
Wisteria sinensis	✓	–	✓	✓	–
Yucca filamentosa 'Bright Edge'	–	✓	–	–	–

Table 3 – Shrubs for Special Situations

From left to right the special situations columns read: walls and fences; hedges; shaded sites; town; coast; and cold sites.

When looking for shrubs for a shaded spot, pick out those with a tick in the shade column.

Table 3 Shrubs for Special Situations						
	Walls and Fences	Hedges	Shaded Sites	Towns	Coast	Cold Sites
Abelia × grandiflora	✓	–	–	✓	✓	–
Abutilon megapotamicum	✓	–	–	✓	–	–
Acer palmatum 'Dissectum Atropurpureum'	–	–	✓	✓	–	–
Actinidia kolomikta	✓	–	–	✓	–	–
Aesculus parviflora	–	–	✓	✓	✓	✓
Artemisia 'Powis castle'	✓	–	–	✓	✓	–
Aucuba japonica 'Crotonifolia'	–	✓	✓	✓	✓	✓
Berberis darwinii	–	✓	✓	✓	✓	✓
Buddleia davidii 'Royal Red'	✓	–	–	✓	✓	–
Buxus sempervirens	–	✓	✓	✓	✓	✓
Callicarpa bodinieri 'Profusion'	✓	–	–	✓	–	–
Camellia japonica 'Elegans'	✓	–	✓	✓	–	–
Campsis radicans	✓	–	–	✓	✓	–
Caryopteris × clandonensis	✓	–	–	✓	✓	–
Ceanothus 'Topaz'	✓	–	–	✓	✓	–
Chaenomeles × superba 'Knaphill Scarlet'	✓	–	✓	✓	✓	✓

Table 3 Shrubs for Special Situations

	Walls and Fences	Hedges	Shaded Sites	Towns	Coast	Cold Sites
Chimonanthus 'Grandiflorus'	✓	–	–	✓	–	–
Choisya ternata	✓	–	✓	✓	–	–
Cistus × corbariensis	✓	–	–	–	✓	–
Clematis 'Lasurstern'	✓	–	–	✓	✓	–
Convolvulus cneorum	–	–	–	–	✓	–
Cornus alba 'Sibirica'	–	✓	✓	✓	✓	✓
Corylopsis pauciflora	✓	–	✓	✓	–	–
Cotinus coggygria 'Royal Purple'	–	–	–	✓	–	–
Cotoneaster conspicuus decorus	–	–	✓	✓	–	✓
Cytisus 'Andreanus'	–	–	–	✓	✓	–
Danae racemosa	–	–	✓	✓	–	–
Daphne mezereum	✓	–	–	✓	✓	✓
Deutzia × 'Mont Rose'	–	✓	✓	✓	✓	✓
Elaeagnus pungens 'Maculata'	–	✓	✓	✓	✓	–
Enkianthus campanulatus	–	–	✓	✓	–	–
Escallonia 'Donard Brilliance'	–	✓	–	✓	✓	–
Euonymus fortunei 'Emerald n Gold'	–	✓	✓	✓	✓	–
Forsythia 'Lynwood'	–	✓	✓	✓	–	✓
Fuchsia 'Riccartonii'	✓	✓	✓	✓	✓	–
Garrya elliptica	✓	–	✓	✓	–	–
Genista lydia	–	–	–	✓	✓	–
Halimium ocymoides	–	–	–	–	✓	–
Hamamelis mollis	✓	–	✓	✓	–	–
Hebe × franciscana 'Blue Gem'	–	✓	✓	✓	✓	–
Hedera helix 'Goldheart'	✓	–	✓	✓	✓	✓
Helianthemum 'Firedragon'	–	–	–	–	✓	–
Hibiscus syriacus 'Woodbridge'	✓	–	–	✓	–	–
Hippophae rhamnoides	–	✓	–	–	✓	✓
Hydrangea macrophylla 'Blue Wave'	–	–	✓	✓	✓	–
Hypericum calycinum	–	–	✓	✓	✓	✓
Ilex aquifolium 'Madame Briot'	–	✓	✓	✓	✓	✓
Jasminum nudiflorum	✓	–	✓	✓	✓	✓
Kalmia latifolia	–	–	–	–	–	–
Kerria japonica 'Pleniflora'	✓	–	✓	✓	✓	–
Kolkwitzia amabilis 'Pink Cloud'	✓	–	–	✓	✓	–
Lavandula 'Hidcote'	–	✓	–	✓	✓	–
Leptospermum scoparium 'Red Damask'	✓	–	–	✓	✓	–
Leucothoe fontanesiana 'Rainbow'	✓	–	✓	✓	–	–
Leycesteria formosa	–	–	✓	✓	–	–
Ligustrum ovalifolium 'Aureum'	–	✓	✓	✓	✓	✓
Lonicera periclymenum 'Belgica'	✓	–	✓	✓	–	–
Magnolia × soulangiana 'Lennei'	–	–	–	✓	–	–
Mahonia aquifolium	–	✓	✓	✓	✓	✓
Myrtus communis	✓	✓	–	✓	✓	–
Nandina domestica	–	–	–	✓	✓	–
Olearia haastii	–	✓	✓	✓	✓	–
Osmanthus delavayi	–	–	–	✓	✓	–
Pachysandra terminalis 'Variegata'	–	–	✓	✓	–	–
Parthenocissus henryana	✓	–	✓	✓	✓	–
Passiflora caerulea	✓	–	–	✓	–	–
Pernettya 'Mother of Pearl'	–	–	✓	✓	–	✓
Perovskia × 'Blue Spire'	–	–	–	✓	✓	–
Philadelphus 'Belle Etoile'	–	✓	✓	✓	✓	✓

Table 3　Shrubs for Special Situations

	Walls and Fences	Hedges	Shaded Sites	Towns	Coast	Cold Sites
Phormium 'Maori Maiden'	✓	–	–	–	✓	–
Photinia × fraseri 'Red Robin'	–	✓	✓	✓	–	–
Physocarpus 'Dart's Gold'	–	–	✓	✓	–	–
Pieris 'Forest Flame'	–	–	✓	✓	–	–
Pittosporum tenuifolium	✓	✓	–	✓	✓	–
Potentilla fruticosa 'Jackman's Variety'	–	✓	✓	✓	✓	–
Prunus triloba	✓	–	–	✓	–	–
Pyracantha 'Orange Glow'	✓	✓	✓	✓	✓	✓
Rhododendron yakushimanum	–	✓	✓	✓	–	✓
Ribes sanguineum 'Pulborough Scarlet'	–	✓	✓	✓	✓	✓
Robinia hispida 'Rosea'	✓	–	–	✓	✓	–
Rosmarinus officinalis 'Miss Jessop's Variety'	–	✓	–	✓	✓	–
Ruta graveolens 'Jackman's Blue'	–	–	✓	✓	✓	–
Salix lanata	–	–	✓	✓	✓	✓
Salvia officinalis 'Purpurascens'	–	–	–	✓	✓	–
Sambucus racemosus 'Sutherland'	–	–	✓	✓	✓	✓
Santolina chamaecyparissus	–	✓	–	✓	✓	–
Senecio 'Sunshine'	–	✓	–	–	✓	–
Skimmia japonica 'Rubella'	–	–	✓	✓	–	✓
Spartium junceum	–	–	–	✓	✓	–
Spiraea × bumalda 'Anthony Waterer'	–	✓	✓	✓	✓	✓
Stranvaesia davidiana	–	–	✓	✓	–	–
Symphoricarpos rivularis	–	✓	✓	✓	–	✓
Syringa velutina (syn *s. palibiniana*)	–	✓	–	✓	✓	–
Tamarix pentandra 'Pink Cascade'	✓	✓	–	✓	✓	–
Viburnum tinus	✓	✓	✓	✓	✓	–
Vinca minor 'Variegata'	–	–	✓	✓	–	–
Vitis coignetiae	✓	–	–	✓	–	–
Weigela florida 'Variegata'	–	–	✓	✓	✓	–
Wisteria sinensis	✓	–	–	✓	✓	–
Yucca filamentosa 'Bright Edge'	–	–	–	✓	✓	–

Table 4 – Shrubs for Special Soils

While most shrubs will grow satisfactorily on average loam soils which are neither over-acid nor over-alkaline, some have special needs and others are especially tolerant.

An example: shrubs like rhododendrons, with a strong preference for acid soils, will not tolerate alkaline soil under any circumstances. But there are some shrubs which are tolerant of acid as well as alkaline soils – cotoneaster is a good example. It is not accidental that some shrubs appear in both the acid and the alkaline soil columns.

Table 4　Shrubs for Special Soils

	Acid	Alkaline	Clay	Sand	Container
Abelia × grandiflora	–	✓	–	✓	✓
Abutilon megapotamicum	–	–	–	–	✓
Acer palmatum 'Dissectum Atropurpureum'	✓	–	✓	–	✓
Actinidia kolomikta	✓	–	–	✓	–

Table 4 Shrubs for Special Soils

	Acid	Alkaline	Clay	Sand	Container
Aesculus parviflora	✓	✓	✓	−	−
Artemisia 'Powis Castle'	✓	✓	−	✓	✓
Aucuba japonica 'Crotonifolia'	✓	✓	✓	−	✓
Berberis darwinii	✓	✓	✓	✓	✓
Buddleia davidii 'Royal Red'	−	✓	−	✓	−
Buxus sempervirens	−	✓	✓	✓	✓
Callicarpa bodinieri 'Profusion'	✓	−	✓	−	✓
Camellia japonica 'Elegans'	✓	−	✓	−	✓
Campsis radicans	−	✓	✓	−	−
Caryopteris × *clandonensis*	−	✓	−	✓	✓
Caenothus 'Topaz'	−	✓	−	✓	✓
Chaenomeles × *superba* 'Knaphill Scarlet'	✓	✓	✓	−	−
Chimonanthus 'Grandiflorus'	✓	✓	−	−	−
Choisya ternata	✓	−	✓	−	✓
Cistus × *corbariensis*	✓	✓	−	✓	✓
Clematis 'Lasurstern'	−	✓	−	✓	−
Convolvulus cneorum	−	✓	−	✓	✓
Cornus alba 'Sibirica'	✓	✓	✓	✓	−
Corylopsis pauciflora	✓	−	✓	−	✓
Cotinus coggygria 'Royal Purple'	−	✓	✓	✓	✓
Cotoneaster conspicuus decorus	✓	✓	✓	✓	✓
Cytisus 'Andreanus'	✓	✓	−	✓	−
Danae racemosa	−	−	✓	−	✓
Daphne mezereum	−	✓	✓	−	−
Deutzia × 'Mont Rose'	✓	✓	✓	−	✓
Elaeagnus pungens 'Maculata'	✓	✓	✓	✓	✓
Enkianthus campanulatus	✓	−	✓	−	−
Escallonia 'Donard Brilliance'	✓	✓	✓	✓	✓
Euonymus fortunei 'Emerald n Gold'	✓	✓	✓	✓	✓
Forsythia 'Lynwood'	✓	✓	✓	✓	−
Fuchsia 'Riccartonii'	✓	−	✓	✓	✓
Garrya elliptica	✓	✓	✓	−	✓
Genista lydia	✓	✓	−	✓	✓
Halimium ocymoides	−	✓	−	✓	−
Hamamelis mollis	✓	−	✓	−	−
Hebe × *franciscana* 'Blue Gem'	−	✓	−	✓	✓
Hedera helix 'Goldheart'	✓	✓	✓	✓	✓
Helianthemum 'Firedragon'	−	✓	−	✓	−
Hibiscus syriacus 'Woodbridge'	✓	✓	−	✓	✓
Hippophae rhamnoides	✓	✓	−	✓	✓
Hydrangea macrophylla 'Blue Wave'	✓	✓	✓	−	✓
Hypericum calycinum	✓	✓	✓	✓	−
Ilex aquifolium 'Madame Briot'	✓	✓	✓	−	−
Jasminum nudiflorum	✓	✓	✓	−	−
Kalmia latifolia	✓	−	✓	−	−
Kerria japonica 'Pleniflora'	✓	✓	✓	−	−
Kolkwitzia amabilis 'Pink Cloud'	✓	−	−	✓	✓
Lavandula 'Hidcote'	✓	✓	−	✓	✓
Leptospermum scoparium 'Red Damask'	✓	−	−	✓	✓
Leucothoe fontanesiana 'Rainbow'	✓	−	−	−	✓
Leycesteria formosa	−	✓	✓	−	−
Ligustrum ovalifolium 'Aureum'	✓	✓	✓	✓	✓
Lonicera periclymenum 'Belgica'	✓	✓	−	−	−
Magnolia × *soulangiana* 'Lennei'	✓	−	✓	−	−

Table 4 Shrubs for Special Soils

	Acid	Alkaline	Clay	Sand	Container
Mahonia aquifolium	✓	✓	✓	–	✓
Myrtus communis	–	✓	–	✓	✓
Nandina domestica	✓	–	–	✓	✓
Olearia haastii	✓	✓	✓	✓	–
Osmanthus delavayi	✓	✓	✓	–	✓
Pachysandra terminalis 'Variegata'	✓	–	–	–	–
Parthenocissus henryana	✓	✓	–	–	–
Passiflora caerulea	✓	✓	–	–	✓
Pernettya 'Mother of Pearl'	✓	–	✓	–	–
Perovskia × 'Blue Spire'	–	✓	–	✓	–
Philadelphus 'Belle Etoile'	✓	✓	✓	–	–
Phormium 'Maori Maiden'	–	✓	–	✓	✓
Photinia × fraseri 'Red Robin'	✓	✓	✓	–	–
Physocarpus 'Dart's Gold'	–	–	–	–	✓
Pieris 'Forest Flame'	✓	–	–	–	✓
Pittosporum tenuifolium	–	✓	–	✓	✓
Potentilla fruticosa 'Jackman's Variety'	✓	✓	–	✓	✓
Prunus triloba	–	✓	–	–	✓
Pyracantha 'Orange Glow'	✓	✓	✓	–	✓
Rhododendron yakushimanum	✓	–	✓	–	✓
Ribes sanguineum 'Pulborough Scarlet'	✓	✓	✓	–	✓
Robinia hispida 'Rosea'	✓	✓	✓	–	✓
Rosmarinus officinalis 'Miss Jessop's Variety'	–	✓	–	✓	✓
Ruta graveolens 'Jackman's Blue'	✓	✓	–	✓	–
Salix lanata	✓	✓	✓	–	–
Salvia officinalis 'Purpurascens'	–	✓	–	✓	✓
Sambucus racemosus 'Sutherland'	✓	✓	✓	–	–
Santolina chamaecyparissus	✓	✓	–	✓	✓
Senecio 'Sunshine'	✓	✓	–	✓	✓
Skimmia japonica 'Rubella'	✓	✓	✓	–	✓
Spartium junceum	✓	✓	–	✓	–
Spiraea × bumalda 'Anthony Waterer'	✓	✓	–	✓	✓
Stranvaesia davidiana	✓	–	✓	–	✓
Symphoricarpos rivularis	✓	✓	–	✓	–
Syringa velutina (syn s. palibiniana)	–	✓	✓	–	✓
Tamarix pentandra 'Pink Cascade'	–	✓	✓	✓	✓
Viburnum tinus	–	✓	✓	–	✓
Vinca minor 'Variegata'	✓	✓	✓	–	✓
Vitis coignetiae	✓	–	✓	–	–
Weigela florida 'Variegata'	✓	✓	✓	–	✓
Wisteria sinensis	✓	✓	–	–	✓
Yucca filamentosa 'Bright Edge'	–	✓	–	✓	✓

Abutilon megapotamicum (Flowering Maple)

- Semi-evergreen
- Hardiness – H2–H3
- Care – Above average

Description Height and spread 6ft(1.8m) when wall trained. An uncommon shrub of lax arching habit and softwood, reasonably quick growing, semi-twining stems. Moderately large dark green leaves. Pendulous red and gold flowers with prominent purple stamens are produced in steady succession from May to October.

Maturity Early maturing – flowers within a year of planting.

Lifespan 8–10 years.

Other varieties A.m. 'Variegatum' – a stronger grower with golden variegated leaves and a height and spread of 8ft(2.5m).

Uses An excellent wall shrub; a useful bush or container shrub.

Planting Set out in spring.

Position Wall train against a sunny south or west wall allowing a 3ft(90cm) spread. In mild climate areas does well in a warm, sheltered border given the protection of other shrubs. Alternatively grow in a 1ft(30cm) container on a sunny, sheltered patio.

Soil Best on free-draining light to medium soils of average fertility. Avoid cold wet clays or extremes of acidity or alkalinity. Use soil-based potting compost in containers.

Propagation Take semi-ripewood node or heel cuttings from June to early August. Set singly in small pots and root in warmth at 60°F(16°C) minimum.

Treatment Protect young plants from wind and frost especially before and immediately after planting. Train up against a wall or other support.

Pruning PG7. Restrain by tipping back in autumn. Cut back frosted shoots to sound wood in spring. Thin out overcrowded shoots as soon as flowering is over for the season.

Problems Occasional attacks from scale insects and mealy bugs.

Fig 52 Given a warm sunny wall and a mild climate Abutilon megapotamicum *will keep up a succession of flowers throughout the summer.*

Acer palmatum 'Dissectum Atropurpureum' (Japanese Maple)

- Deciduous
- Hardiness – H2
- Care – Average

Description Height 3½ft(1m) Spread 5ft(1.5m). An outstanding very slow-growing choice foliage shrub with a dense mushroom-like outline becoming rounded with age. The finely cut, much divided purple leaves are a feature from spring until autumn when they turn red before leaf fall.

Maturity Foliage interest from planting.

Lifespan 40 years given good growing conditions.

Other varieties A.p. 'Dissectum' – delightful

with green leaves and red autumn tints. *A.p.* 'Dissectum Crimson Queen' – striking blood red foliage. *A.p.* 'Dissectum Nigrum' – dark purple summer foliage.

Uses A particularly good rock garden or waterside specimen. A good patio container shrub.

Planting Plant in spring; or autumn in very mild areas.

Position Choose a sunny position shielded from strong midday sun. Avoid exposed wind-swept sites and those liable to regular late spring frosts. Allow an initial 2½ft(75cm) spread, then increase as growth is made.

Soil Needs a cool, moist, organic rich acid or neutral soil. Avoid badly drained clay soils and alkaline conditions. Use lime-free soil-based potting compost in containers.

Propagation Graft in spring onto *Acer palmatum* rootstocks. Keep in cool, shaded position indoors for about eight weeks until the graft has taken. Harden off gradually and give winter protection for the first few years. Sow *Acer palmatum* for rootstocks in October. Chill out-doors until February. Then germinate at 60°F(16°C).

Fig 53 The finely divided bronze-purple summer foliage of Acer palmatum *'Dissectum Atropurpureum' (Japanese Maple) is followed by superb autumn tints. For best results, give it a sheltered spot out of the wind.*

Treatment Keep young plants well watered and mulched in dry weather. In hard water areas use rainwater for container grown shrubs. Protect from cold and drying winds.

Pruning PG5. Minimal – shorten straggly shoots in autumn.

Problems In warm dry conditions red spider mite can be a nuisance. Leaf scorch and tip burn due to wind and/or frost.

Actinida kolomikta (Kolomikta Vine)

- Deciduous climber
- Hardiness – H2–H3
- Care – Average

Description Height 20ft(6m) unrestricted. Spread variable – up to 10ft(3m). A choice, relatively uncommon, quick growing climber of slender twining habit. Unusual green, white and pink blotched variegated leaves provide interest from late spring to autumn. Female plants produce insignificant fragrant white summer flowers followed by yellow, edible fruits. Leaf variegation less pronounced than with male plants.

Maturity Starts to flower in 2–3 years.

Lifespan 40 years plus in favourable situations.

Other varieties *A. chinensis* (Chinese Gooseberry) Hardier and more vigorous than *A. kolomikta* reaching 30ft(9m) in height. Grown for its edible green gooseberry-like fruits which turn brown when ripe. Large green leaves and hairy reddish brown stems.

Uses *A. kolomikta* makes a good ornamental climber.

Planting Set out in spring or autumn. Plant direct or in containers, 1½ft(45cm) minimum depth and diameter.

Position A warm, sunny south or west wall is needed and allow 5ft(1.5m) minimum between plants. To ensure flowers and fruit with the Chinese gooseberry set out in full sun and plant both male and female plants.

Soil Deep fertile free-draining soil – avoid cold wet clays and shallow impoverished soils. Use rich soil-based potting compost in containers.

Fig 54   *The foliage colour of this climber* Actinidia kolomikta, *is best on a warm sunny wall.*

Propagation   Take semi-ripewood cuttings during summer and root under cover. Can be raised from seed but results are unpredictable and normally inferior to cuttings.

Treatment   Protect newly planted young climbers from drought, cold, wind and frost. Train up wall supports.

Pruning   PG7. Restrict plants to allotted space and thin out weak, overcrowded shoots in autumn or late winter.

Problems   Generally trouble free.

Aucuba japonica 'Crotonifolia' (Aucuba)

- Evergreen shrub
- Hardiness – HI–H2
- Care – Easy

Description   Height and spread 7–10ft(2–3m) unrestricted but can be restrained. An outstanding hardy shrub, grown mainly for the beauty of its foliage and for its reliability and ease of cultivation in a wide range of differing situations. The large glossy, leathery green leaves are spotted and splashed with gold and are the main attraction of this dense, bushy shrub.

Maturity   Foliage effects from planting.

Lifespan   40 years plus.

Other varieties   *A.j.* 'Picturata' – more prominent gold spotted leaves than the above, and grows better in strong sun; *A.j.* 'Variegata' – similar to above; *A.j.* 'Salicifolia' – plain green narrow leaves.

Uses   A versatile shrub suitable for beds and borders in town, coast or country. Ideal for planting under trees, as a focal point and as a specimen. Well suited to tubs, urns and even windowboxes when small.

Planting   Set out during autumn or spring.

Position   Partial shade is ideal. If possible, avoid east-facing positions.

Fig 55 Aucuba 'Crotonifolia' with its bold foliage is a reliable medium-sized shrub giving year-round interest. It grows in most soils and sites.

Soil Adaptable, but does best in moist reasonably deep soil of average fertility. Avoid extremes of acidity or alkalinity. Tolerant of fertile clay soils.

Propagation Take semi-ripewood heel cuttings in August or September and root under cover. Provided variations in progeny are acceptable, sow seed in October. Chill and germinate in warmth 65°F(18°C) in spring.

Treatment Protect newly set out autumn planted shrubs from cold drying winds during their first winter and spring.

Pruning PG5. Little pruning is needed beyond shortening shoots in summer to maintain shape. Old overgrown shrubs can be rejuvenated by hard cutting back in summer.

Problems Relatively trouble free.

Berberis darwinii (Barberry)

- Evergreen shrub
- Hardiness – HI
- Care – Easy to average

Description Height 8ft(2.5m) or more. Spread 5ft(1.5m) or more. A first rate, dense, bushy, semi-vigorous flowering evergreen shrub.

Clusters of small crimson-tinged yellow-orange fragrant flowers are freely produced along slender branches during April and May. Currant sized blue-purple berries follow in summer. Small, prickly dark-green glossy leaves are pleasing year round and make an excellent contrast to the spring flowers.

Maturity Expect flowering and berrying within 1 or 2 years of planting.

Lifespan 30 years plus given favourable conditions.

Other varieties *B. x stenophylla* Height 10ft(3m), spread 6ft(1.8m). A fine dense thicket forming evergreen shrub with golden spring flowers and blue-black summer berries. The dark green leaves are narrow and glossy. Quick growing. Maturity and lifespan as *B. darwinii*. *B. thunbergii* 'Atropurpurea', height 6ft(1.8m), spread 4ft(1.2m). An attractive thicket-forming deciduous shrub. The bronze-red foliage turns bright red just before leaf fall in autumn. Clusters of yellow spring flowers are followed by blood red late summer berries. Growth rate, maturity and lifespan as *B. darwinii*.

Uses Suited to formal and semi-formal treat-

Fig 56 Evergreen berberis grows well in most gardens – renowned for its year-round interest and spring colour.

ment in borders and as hedging. Makes a good specimen planted direct or in a container.

Planting Set out in autumn or spring. Resents root disturbance so use container-grown stock.

Position Suited to sun or semi-shade. Avoid full exposure to freezing and drying east or north winds.

Soil Moist fertile not over-rich loam preferred but adapts to almost any soil of average fertility. Avoid extremes of acidity or alkalinity, or wet soils.

Propagation Take semi-ripewood heel or node cuttings in July or August. Root under cover.

Treatment Unfussy.

Pruning PG2 for semi-formal effects. Or PG6 for a clipped look and formal hedging.

Problems Occasionally tends to be subject to attack by aphids.

Fig 57 Buddleia davidii 'Harlequin', *with its variegated foliage is an excellent shrub for alkaline soils.*

Buddleia davidii 'Royal Red' (Butterfly Bush)

- Deciduous shrub
- Hardiness – H2
- Care – Easy to average

Description Height and spread 10ft(3m). A popular, quick growing, flowering deciduous shrub attractive to butterflies. Masses of tiny purple-red flowers are carried in long, fragrant, terminal spikes during July and August. The leaves are long and green with a greyish white felted reverse.

Maturity Begins flowering within 1 or 2 years of planting.

Lifespan Best replaced after 10–15 years.

Other varieties *B.d.* 'Black Knight' – dark

purple. *B.d.* 'Empire Blue' – violet-blue. *B.d.* 'Peace' – white. Colours apart these three varieties are similar to *B.d.* 'Royal Red'. A near relative *B. alternifolia* – height 8ft(2.5m) and spread 6ft(1.8m) makes a first class bush or standard. It has slender arching branches and purple flowers in June.

Uses Excellent as a wall shrub; as an accent shrub in the border; and as a free-standing specimen focal point. Popular with flower arrangers. Good at the coast.

Planting Set out in autumn or early winter – or during spring – allow at least a 7ft(2m) spread.

Position Open warm, sunny situations which are not too exposed to strong winds are favoured.

Soil Prefers a medium to light soil which is fertile but not over-rich. Tolerant of moderately alkaline conditions.

Propagation Take semi-ripe heel or node cuttings in July or August and root under cover.

Treatment Shorten back the tops of newly set out shrubs by half to two thirds.

Pruning PG3. Cut flowered wood hard back in autumn or late winter.

Problems Relatively trouble free.

Buxus sempervirens (Box)

- Evergreen shrub or tree
- Hardiness – H1–H2
- Care - Easy

Description Height 20ft(6m) or more if unchecked. Spread to 7ft(2m) and over if unchecked. Slow growing reaches 7ft(2m) in ten years. Makes a dense much branched rounded shrub or broadly columnar tree. The small glossy, dark green, aromatic leaves which form a close textured surface, are a major feature. Insignificant small yellow flowers appear in April.

Maturity Year round foliage interest from planting time onwards.

Lifespan 100 years plus for direct planted shrubs – much less for container plants.

Other varieties *B.s.* 'Elegantissima' – a dome-

shaped variegated dwarf form of the above. Height 4ft((1.2m). Leaves are margined creamy white. *B.s.* 'Suffruticosa' – the traditional edging box. A diminutive form of *B. sempervirens* – height to 2ft(60cm).

Uses Widely used for hedging and screening providing a backdrop for flower beds. Excellent for topiary. Good in containers as well as in beds and borders. Makes a useful specimen tree or shrub.

Planting Set out in autumn or spring. Space hedging plants 1ft(30cm) apart. Allow single specimens 3½ft(1m) minimum spread.

Position Sun or semi-shade are suitable. Avoid direct exposure to freezing strong east or north winds.

Soil Light to medium soils preferred but adapts to most free-draining soils of average fertility including alkaline. Dislikes cold wet heavy land.

Propagation Take semi-ripe heel or node cuttings from July to early September and root under cover.

Treatment Protect newly set out shrubs from strong winds and frost during their first winter.

Pruning PG6. Clip to shape during late spring or summer.

Problems Occasionally attacked by the Box sucker pest, but otherwise normally trouble free.

Callicarpa bodinieri 'Profusion' (Beauty Berry)

- Deciduous shrub
- Hardiness H2–H3
- Care – Easy to average

Description Height to 7ft(2m). Spread 5ft(1.5m) or more. A medium to slow growing stiffly erect, berrying shrub noted for its autumn tints and fruits. The clusters of insignificant pale pink June flowers are followed by masses of bright rose-purple autumn berries persisting on bare branches into winter. The green summer foliage turns to attractive rose, pink, red and gold shades in autumn.

Maturity Starts berrying within 2–3 years.

Lifespan   At least 15 years.

Other varieties   The closely related *C.B. giraldii* is a slightly smaller shrub – 6ft(1.8m) by 4ft(1.2m). Rosy purple June flowers are followed by dark lilac autumn berries and leaf tints.

Uses   An uncommon but effective wall or border shrub with a difference, providing a focal point or accent plant during autumn and winter.

Planting   Set out in autumn, early winter or spring allowing a minimum 3½ft(1m) spread.

Position   Select a sunny, sheltered spot backed by a wall or screened by shrubs to give protection from cold north and east winds. For maximum berrying, plant in groups of two or three.

Soil   An acid or neutral moist, but free-draining, fertile peaty or leafy soil is best. Avoid shallow chalk or alkaline soils.

Propagation   Take semi-ripe heel or node cuttings in July and root at 60–65°F(16–18°C).

Treatment   Give newly set out plants wind and frost protection during their first winter.

Pruning   PG5. Cut out old and useless overcrowded shoots in spring before growth starts.

Problems   Usually trouble free.

Camellia japonica 'Elegans' (Camellia)

- Evergreen shrub
- Hardiness H2–H3
- Care – Easy to average

Description   Height and spread ultimately 10ft(3m) but normally slow growing to about

Fig 58   Varieties of Camellia japonica *normally produce a profusion of spring blooms – which are seen to advantage against the bold evergreen leaves.*

5ft(1.5m) in ten years. An outstanding, choice flowering and foliage shrub of rounded or spreading habit. Large salmon pink double blooms normally appear in March and April. They are set off to advantage by the large bold glossy leaves.

Maturity   Expect flowering to start within 2–3 years.

Lifespan   35 years for direct planted shrubs, less for container stock.

Other varieties   *C.j.* 'Adolph Audussen' – semi-double large red flowers with golden stamens. *C.j.* 'Alba Plena' – large double white blooms.

Uses   Makes a good free-standing specimen as a focal point in grass or patio area. Also suitable for mixed planting with such as rhododendrons and azaleas. Try it as a wall plant or in a container.

Planting   Plant direct or containerize during mild weather in autumn or spring, allowing a minimum 5ft(1.5m) spread.

Position   A partly shaded spot, sheltered from cold wind, with a west or even north-facing aspect and backed by a wall or shrubs or light tree canopy, will suit. Avoid east-facing sites liable to early morning sun and subsequent quick thaws after overnight frost.

Soil   Moist leafy well-drained acid or near neutral soil that is lime-free, but not too rich is needed. Use lime-free potting compost in containers.

Propagation   Take semi-ripe heel cuttings in July and root in warmth. Alternatively peg down layers in September.

Treatment   Protect newly set out shrubs from wind especially during their first winter. Insulate roots of young plants from frost.

Pruning   PG5. Negligible other than to shorten any frosted shoots to shape in late spring.

Problems   Occasionally attacked by mealy bugs or scale insects. Bud drop or frost damage can occur.

Campsis radicans (Trumpet Vine)

- Deciduous climber
- Hardiness – H3
- Care – Above average

Description   Height 25ft(7.5m). Spread 15ft (4.5m). A very vigorous, self-clinging climber grown for its spectacular flowers. Clusters of orange-scarlet trumpet shaped blooms are produced during August and September midst deep green foliage.

Maturity   Flowering starts at 4–5 years old.

Lifespan   40 years plus.

Other varieties   *C.r.* 'Flava' – a yellow flowered lookalike.

Uses   Excellent for large expanses of wall and fencing and for training over pergolas or rafters.

Planting   Set out plants in spring. Reserve autumn planting for exceptionally sheltered mild winter areas. Allow a minimum 10ft(3m) of wall space.

Position   A sunny south wall is best but a west facing aspect in full sun will do. Only attempt to train over a pergola in very mild climates.

Soil   A well-drained, deep fertile soil that is neither very acid nor highly alkaline should suffice.

Propagation   Root semi-ripe cuttings in warmth during July. Alternatively peg down layers in autumn or spring.

Treatment   Keep well watered during first summer. Do not allow to grow direct onto masonry – tie in and train over trellis. Spray the foliage with water in the evening of hot days to discourage red spider.

Pruning   PG2 and PG7. Thin out weak, over-crowded and flowered shoots in late autumn. Shorten back overlong growths at the same time.

Problems   Subject to attacks by red spider mites and scale insects.

Caryopteris × clandonensis
(Blue Spiraea)

- Deciduous shrub
- Hardiness – H2–H3
- Care – Average to above average

Description   Height and spread about 3ft(90cm). A first class low growing rounded shrub of bushy habit for mild climate areas. Pleasing violet blue flowers are carried on slender branches from August to October and are attractive to bees. The aromatic grey green summer foliage is an added bonus. Quick growing.

Maturity Flowers and reaches full height within 12 months of planting.

Lifespan Best renewed after 8–10 years.

Other varieties *C* × *c.* 'Heavenly Blue' – similar to the above but has mid-blue flowers and a more compact habit. *C* × *c.* 'Kew Blue' – darker blue flowers but otherwise looks like *C* × *clandonensis* .

Uses Various – as ground cover; as a wall shrub; in island bed or border; as a container shrub; and for cutting.

Planting Preferably set out in spring with autumn as a second alternative – allow a minimum 2ft(60cm) spread.

Position A warm sunny spot, sheltered from cold winds, ensures best results.

Soil A light to medium well-drained soil of average fertility suits this shrub. Does well on alkaline soil.

Propagation Root semi-ripe cuttings under cover in summer.

Treatment If grown in other than a mild climate area protect the roots and crown from frost.

Pruning PG3. Cut flowered stems hard back to old wood or main frame after flowering in autumn or late winter.

Problems Generally no serious troubles.

Ceanothus 'Topaz'
(Californian Lilac)

- Deciduous shrub
- Hardiness – H2–H3
- Care – Average to above average

Description Height up to 10ft(3m). Spread 8ft(2.5m). A quick growing bushy rounded or spreading shrub. Grown for its clusters of bright mid-blue flowers from late June to October. The leaves are mid-green and rather ordinary.

Fig 59 Ceanothus repens, *seen here as a garden centre plant, is a first-class mound-forming ground cover shrub for a sunny spot.*

Maturity Starts to flower within one or at the most two years of planting.

Lifespan Normally 20 years at least.

Other varieties *C. thyrsiflorus repens* – height 3ft(90cm), spread 8ft(2.5m). A mound-forming evergreen shrub of similar hardiness to above. Mid-blue early summer flowers. Needs minimal pruning.

Uses Grown mainly as a wall shrub. Suitable also as a border shrub and as a formal specimen. Useful for cutting.

Planting Set out in spring or autumn allowing at least 5ft(1.5m) spread.

Position Best on a sunny, sheltered south or west-facing wall. Needs shelter from cold and drying winds.

Soil Needs to be well-drained, of light to medium texture and of average fertility. Avoid alkaline rich conditions.

Propagation Take semi-ripe heel or node cuttings in summer and root under cover.

Treatment Protect newly set out shrubs from wind and frost – vital during their first winter.

Pruning PG3. Ideally, restrict the shrub size to a maximum height and spread of about 6ft(1.8m) by pruning flowered shoots back to the main framework after flowering in autumn or late winter.

Problems Liable to attack by scale insects. Prone to frost damage in all but the mildest areas. Suffers from chlorosis if grown on alkaline soils.

Chaenomeles superba 'Knaphill Scarlet' (Flowering Quince)

- Deciduous shrub
- Hardiness – HI–H2
- Care – Average

Description Height and spread 4–5ft(1.2–1.5m) as a free-standing shrub. Expect height and spread to double when wall trained in a warm garden but somewhat variable in size. A spreading vigorous, popular flowering shrub with interlacing stems and branches. Bright red pea-sized buds appear on bare branches during winter. They open in succession from March to May into large salmon scarlet apple blossom like flowers. Greenish yellow apple or pear shaped fruits follow in autumn. The leaves are mid-green and ordinary.

Maturity Flowering starts within 2–3 years of planting.

Lifespan 30 years at least.

Other varieties C × s. 'Pink Lady' – pink flowers and C × s. 'Rowallane' – large red flowers. Flower colour apart these two varieties are similar to the above.

Uses Very good as a wall shrub, effective as a free-standing border shrub and as ground cover on banks. Useful for cutting.

Planting Ideally set out in late autumn or early winter. Next best is late winter or early spring. Allow a minimum 3ft(90cm) spread per plant.

Position Good in sun or shade and adapts to most aspects as a wall plant. Avoid full exposure to freezing easterly spring winds or early morning sun.

Soil Almost any fertile soil will suffice including clay if well drained. Tolerates alkaline conditions.

Propagation Root semi-ripe node cuttings in summer, or peg down layers in summer.

Treatment Tie in wall plants as they grow.

Pruning PG2 and PG7. Summer prune by cutting back side growths to 2 or 3 leaves. If shy flowering brutt in summer.

Problems Liable to bud stripping by birds in hard winters. Subject to fireblight disease.

Choisya ternata (Mexican Orange Blossom)

- Evergreen shrub
- Hardiness – H2
- Care – Easy to average

Description Height to 7ft(2m) and over – slightly wider than tall. A rounded average to slow growing bushy shrub with striking foliage and immense floral beauty. Clusters of white, sweetly scented starlike flowers appear in April and May continuing intermittently until late summer. While giving year round interest, the glossy aromatic dark green leaves provide an excellent foil for the flowers.

Maturity Flowering begins within 2 years of planting.

Lifespan 15 years plus.

Other varieties C.t. 'Sundance' – a golden

Fig 60 Choisya has sweetly scented flowers and does well in sun or light shade.

Fig 61 Choisya 'Sundance' is a choice golden evergreen form of the popular fragrant flowered Mexican orange. The young plant shown here will eventually make a small to medium sized shrub.

leaved form of the above. If anything it is a shade smaller in height and spread 6ft(1.8m). Foliage colourings are best in full sun.

Uses Looks well in a mixed shrub border in sun; as underplanting in light shade; as a wall shrub; and even as semi-formal hedge provided there is adequate space. A good container shrub. Popular for cutting.

Planting Set out in spring or during autumn allowing a 4ft(1.3m) spread.

Position Must have a warm, sheltered spot in sun or partial shade. Avoid east-facing sites exposed to early morning sun.

Soil A light to medium well-drained peaty or leafy loam of average fertility suits well. Tolerates alkaline conditions provided they are not too extreme and the soil is not too shallow. Minimum container size 12in(30cm).

Treatment Give newly planted shrubs protection from wind and frost – vital during their first winter. The roots of container stock of all ages should be insulated against hard frost.

Pruning PG5. Routine pruning is not as a rule necessary. If pruning is needed do it in summer.

Propagation Root semi-ripe heel or node cuttings under cover in July or August.

Problems Normally trouble free but young plants are prone to frost injury.

Clematis 'Lasurstern' (Virgin's Bower)

- Deciduous climber
- Hardiness – H2–H3
- Care – Average to above average

Description Height up to 10ft(3m). Spread to about 7ft(2m). A bushy quick growing climber noted for its colourful flowers. The very large lavender-blue blooms – up to 5in(13cm) across – appear during May and June to be followed by a second flush in September. The green leaves are ordinary and unspectacular – but incorporate the tendril attachments needed for support.

Maturity Normally flowers in the first season after planting.

Lifespan 10 years or more given care.

Other varieties *C.* 'Nelly Moser'. The striped flowers, with blush white petals, each have a carmine bar radiating out from the centre – rather like a star. In other respects, similar to the above.

Uses Essentially for covering walls, fences, sheds, pergolas and arches. Also effective for carpeting banks as a form of summer ground cover.

Planting Set out in May or alternatively in September allowing a minimum 4ft(1.2m) spread of wall space. Plant amongst dwarf shrubs or herbaceous plants to shade roots and ensure a cool, moist root run. Allow an area of at least 5×5ft(1.5×1.5m) for ground cover treatment.

Position A sheltered but open south, west or east aspect will suit.

Soil Aim to ensure a cool, deep, moist, well-drained, fertile alkaline loam.

Propagation Root semi-ripe node cuttings under cover in July. Alternatively pin down tip layers of new growths in summer.

Treatment Train and tie in to supports.

Pruning PG2 or PG3. Shorten the main stem

Fig 62 Clematis 'Nellie Moser' is a highly popular large-flowered clematis. Excellent on alkaline soils.

by one third immediately after planting. Where space allows, simply thin out flowered wood in autumn. In restricted spaces cut out all the flowered wood in autumn or late winter.

Problems Aphid and earwigs can attack. Clematis wilt can result in the complete collapse of plants.

Cornus alba 'Sibirica' (Red-barked Dogwood)

● Deciduous shrub
● Hardiness – HI
● Care - Average to above average

Description Height and spread up to about 7ft(2m). A vigorous, wide, spreading, thicket forming, rapid growing shrub renowned for its

brilliant bark. Clusters of small white or greenish-white flowers appear in June followed by whitish autumn berries. The mid-green summer foliage turns to yellow in autumn before dropping to reveal vivid, eyecatching blood-red, sealing wax-like stems for winter interest.

Maturity Expect coloured stems in the first year. The less conspicuous flowers and fruits appear in the second and subsequent years.

Lifespan Up to 20 years and more.

Other varieties *C. stolonifera* 'Flaviramea', the Yellow-barked Dogwood. Similar to the above except that the young bark is butter yellow.

Uses Group plantings in borders or at the waterside where space allows. Singly at the back of mixed borders. Useful for cutting.

Planting Set out in autumn or early winter – or spring – allowing each plant a minimum 3ft(90cm) spread.

Position Good in light to medium partial shade. Adapts to sun if the roots are kept moist.

Soil Moist medium to heavy rich soil preferred. However, will adapt to most soils of average fertility including alkaline. Dislikes hot, dry soils.

Propagation Root semi-ripe heel or node cuttings under cover during summer. Alternatively, pin down layers in September or detach rooted suckers in early winter.

Fig 63 Cornus (Dogwood) grows well on a wide range of soils but are normally at their best on alkaline soils. Variegated varieties prefer sun – for good leaf colour.

Treatment Keep well watered and mulched in the first summer – vital in prolonged dry weather.

Pruning PG4. Cutting down to soil level in April ensures the best bark colourings on new wood.

Problems Normally trouble free.

Cotinus coggygria 'Royal Purple' (Smoke Tree)

- Deciduous shrub
- Hardiness – H2
- Care – Easy to average

Description Height and spread up to about 10ft(3m). Makes an outstanding bushy or rounded, primarily foliage shrub which is moderately quick growing. The flowers and stalks collectively create a purplish haze or smokiness during summer – hence the name 'smoke tree'. The purple summer leaves turn to red in autumn.

Maturity The purple summer leaves provide colour even on young plants. However, it is 3–5 years before the flower haze becomes evident.

Lifespan 25 years plus.

Fig 64 Cotinus coggygria 'Royal Purple' is an outstanding foliage shrub and is a useful accent plant.

Other varieties *C.c.* 'Notcutts Variety' is very similar to the above but has darker leaves and a pinky-purple inflorescence of flowers.

Uses A useful back of the border shrub. A good accent plant. Effective when massed on a large scale.

Planting Set out in autumn/early winter or spring allowing a minimum spread of 6ft(1.8m).

Position Although a sunny spot ensures good leaf colour, this shrub adapts to partial light shade.

Soil Grow in a deep sandy to medium, well-drained fertile but not over-rich soil for the best leaf colourings and autumn tints.

Propagation Peg down layers in September. Alternatively take semi-ripe heel cuttings in summer and root under cover.

Treatment Keep well watered and mulched during the first year until it gets going.

Pruning PG5. Little pruning is needed apart from shortening straggly shoots in late autumn.

Problems Generally trouble free.

Cotoneaster conspicuus decorus (Cotoneaster)

- Evergreen shrub
- Hardiness – H1–H2
- Care – Easy

Description Height to about 2½ft(75cm). Spread approximately 6ft(1.8m). A much branched moderately quick growing low, mound forming shrub with arching branches. White hawthorn-like scented flowers wreathe the branches in May and early June. Globose red berries follow in autumn and persist well into winter. The leaves are glossy dark green with woolly felted undersides.

Maturity Normally flowers and berries within 12 months of planting.

Lifespan Up to 20 years.

Other varieties *C. dammeri* – height to about 8in(20cm) spreading indefinitely. A quick growing, prostrate, evergreen ground hugging shrub. Flowers, berries, maturity and lifespan as above.

Fig 65 *Cotoneaster – a great favourite.*

Fig 66 *Cytisus (Broom) makes a dramatic display.*

Uses Effective as ground cover in beds and borders and when underplanted beneath a tree canopy. Good as a container shrub.

Planting Set out in autumn or spring allowing a minimum spread of 3ft(90cm).

Position Well suited to partial, permanent light or dappled shade but given good soil will adapt to growing in full sun. Avoid full exposure to freezing north or east winds.

Soil Grows well on most soils of average fertility including those of an alkaline nature.

Propagation Root semi-ripe heel or node cuttings under cover in July or August. Alternatively peg down layers in autumn.

Treatment Protect from drying winds during the first winter.

Pruning PG5. Little pruning is needed beyond keeping to allotted space – a job for late spring.

Problems Subject to occasional attacks from aphid, scale insects, woolly aphid and fireblight.

Cytisus 'Andreanus' (Broom)

- Deciduous shrub
- Hardiness – H1–H2
- Care – Easy to average

Description Height and spread up to 6ft(2m) when grown in the open. Height up to 10ft(3m) when grown in shrub border. A colourful, free-flowering, rapidly growing bushy shrub. Masses of gold and brown-crimson pea shaped flowers are carried on slender stems in May and June, to be followed by seed pods in late summer and autumn (see pruning). The green stems are sparsely foliaged in summer and stiffly ascending when not in bloom. The young shoots retain their greenness in winter. Self seeds readily.

Maturity Blooms within 12–24 months of planting.

Lifespan 5–8 years.

Other varieties *C. scoparius* (Common Broom). Very popular with bright yellow scented flowers in May and June. Similar to the above in other respects.

Uses Makes a good accent plant in beds and borders. An excellent nurse plant and/or filler. Also good for stabilizing banks.

Planting This shrub resents root disturbance. So set out very young, pot grown, transplants of under 12 months old and preferably not more than about 8in(20cm) in height. Allow a minimum spread of about 4ft(1.2m).

Position A sunny spot is necessary. Will adapt to any open aspect except northerly.

Soil Does best in free-draining, dryish sandy soil that is low in nitrogen. Avoid alkaline conditions and heavy wet soils.

Propagation Root semi-ripe heel cuttings under cover in August. Can be raised from seeds sown indoors in April but the progeny are likely to be variable and may include 'all yellow' flowers. Those with experience could graft indoors in April onto laburnum rootstocks.

Treatment No special care.

Pruning PGI. Do not neglect to prune or you risk shortening useful life. Never cut back into old wood. Immediately after blooming, cut back flowered shoots hard, avoiding the formation of seed pods which weaken the plant.

Problems Normally trouble free.

Daphne mezereum (Mezereon)

- Deciduous shrub
- Hardiness – HI–H2
- Care – Easy

Description Height and spread about 2½ft(75cm). A popular slow growing, stiffly erect, sparsely branched rounded shrub grown for its flowers and fruits. The clusters of sweetly scented, small pink or purple-red flowers are already blooming in February and March as the leaves start opening. Scarlet autumn berries follow – these are poisonous. The leaves are green and rather ordinary.

Maturity Expect flowering and fruiting on small plants – often within a year of planting.

Lifespan 10–15 years but can be a great deal longer.

Other varieties *D. odora* 'Aureomarginata'. Height 4ft(1.2m), spread 5ft(1.5m). An evergreen rounded shrub with pink early spring flowers and red late summer berries. The leaves are margined creamy-white.

Uses A desirable shrub for planting near doorways and windows to provide colour and fragrance.

Planting Set out in autumn or spring, allow a 2ft(60cm) spread.

Position A warm, sheltered sunny spot is preferred, but will adapt to partial light shade. Avoid cold north or east winds.

Fig 67 The sweet scented pink flower spikes of Daphne mezereum *appear in early spring before the leaves unfold.*

Soil Grows well on free-draining, loamy soil of average fertility and will adapt to alkaline conditions.

Propagation Root semi-ripe heel cuttings under cover in summer.

Treatment No special treatment needed as a rule.

Pruning PG5. Negligible.

Problems Occasional aphid attacks likely. Susceptible to infection by mosaic virus, resulting in mottled leaves and stunted growth.

Elaeagnus pungens 'Maculata' (Oleaster)

- Evergreen
- Hardiness – H2–H3
- Care – Easy to average

Description Height and spread 10ft(3m). One of the very best and brightest foliage shrubs. It is relatively slow growing with a neat, spreading habit. The large, leathery, glossy green leaves are centrally splashed bright golden yellow to give year round appeal. With mature shrubs the insignificant silvery white flowers become conspicuous during late autumn due to the refreshing fragrance.

Maturity Immediate foliage interest. Flowering may be delayed for 4–5 years.

Lifespan 40 years and more.

Other varieties *E. x ebbingei* 'Gilt Edge'. Similar but the green leaves are edged gold.

Uses Very versatile and makes effective hedging and screening; is excellent as a specimen shrub; is a good accent plant in borders, beds and containers; and is popular for cutting for indoors.

Planting Set out in autumn or spring allowing about 2ft(60cm) between hedging plants, 4ft(1.2m) between screening plants, and about a 5ft(1.5m) spread in beds and borders. Use a 12–14in(30–35cm) container.

Position Colours are best in sun but adapts to light partial shade. Avoid planting where exposed to the full blast of freezing north or east winds. Good at coast and in towns.

Fig 68 Elaeagnus 'Maculata' makes a medium sized shrub, suitable for use as either a specimen shrub or for hedging.

Soil Not too fussy. Does well on most soils of average fertility. Prefers free-draining light to medium soils but tolerant of clay and alkaline conditions if drainage is reasonable.

Propagation Root semi-ripe heel or node cuttings under cover in warmth during July or August.

Treatment Keep well watered in first summer after planting.

Pruning PG2 and PG6. Cut newly set out plants back by one third. Thin out overcrowded or weak growths on bushes during late spring or late summer and clip or prune hedges at the same time. Cut out any reverted green shoots on sight.

Problems Occasional reverted green shoots. Otherwise normally trouble free.

Escallonia 'Donard Brilliance'
(Escallonia)

- Evergreen shrub
- Hardiness – H2–H3
- Care – Above average

Description Height and spread to about 6ft(1.8m). A quick growing pleasing flowering shrub of rounded, bushy habit. Rose red flowers are freely produced during summer and look well against the dark green glossy leaves which provide year round interest.

Maturity Expect flowering within a couple of years of planting.

Lifespan 25 years or more.

Other varieties *E.* 'Apple Blossom'. Height and spread to about 5ft(1.5m). Similar to 'Donard Brilliance' but slower growing with pink and white flowers. *E.* 'Red Elf'. Similar to 'Apple Blossom' but with deep crimson flowers.

Uses Pleasing as clipped semi-formal hedging and as screening; good in beds and borders; popular for cutting; and suitable for container growing.

Planting Set out in autumn or spring allowing a 4ft(1.2m) spread. Set hedging shrubs 1½ft(45cm) apart.

93

Fig 69 Escallonia *is a useful summer flowering shrub. It is suitable for hedging and does well at the seaside. It needs a mild winter climate.*

Position Adapts to sun or partial shade. Avoid full exposure to freezing east or north winds and do not plant in cold winter areas. Good in coastal districts.

Soil Grows well in most well-drained soils of average fertility including alkaline and those inclined to be heavy.

Propagation Propagate by rooting semi-ripe heel or node cuttings under cover in July or August.

Treatment Shorten by pruning back the top growth by about one quarter when setting the plants out.

Pruning PG2 and PG6. Thin out bushy shrubs after flowering. Cut hedging and clipped shrubs in June or July.

Problems Trouble free.

Euonymus fortunei 'Emerald 'n' Gold' (Winter Creeper)

- Evergreen Shrub
- Hardiness – HI–H2
- Care – Easy to average

Description Height about 1½ft(45cm). Spread about 2½ft(75cm). A moderately quick growing, widely grown, creeping hummocky, mound forming, leafy foliage shrub. The glossy golden variegated green leaves take on pink shades in severely cold weather to provide year round appeal. Insignificant greenish white flowers appear in late spring on mature plants.

Maturity Instant foliage effects.

Lifespan 20 years and more.

Other varieties *E.* 'Emerald Gaiety'. Height

2ft(60cm). Spread 4ft(1.2m). A silver variegated form similar to 'Emerald'n'Gold', but slightly taller and more vigorous.

Uses Ideal as ground cover and as underplanting. Effective in beds and borders. Useful in tubs and containers, and popular for cutting.

Planting Set out in spring or autumn. Allow a 1½ft(45cm) spread. Set four plants per sq yd/m for quick ground cover. Plunge plant in mixed containers.

Position Grows well in sun or semi-shade. Do not plant on east-facing sites unless there is shade from early morning sun.

Soil Adapts to most free-draining soils of average fertility. Tolerant of alkaline as well as medium to heavy soils.

Propagation Root semi-ripe heel or node cuttings under cover in July or August. Alternatively, peg down layers in spring or autumn.

Treatment Spray over the foliage during prolonged dry weather in the first season.

Pruning Clip over young plants after setting them out to make them bushy. PG5 for semi-formal effect. PG6 and PG7 for clipped formal situations and containment. Aim to prune out frosted or reverted or straggly shoots in late spring or summer. Clip formal bushes and

ground cover at the same time to shape and to restrict to allotted space.

Problems Trouble free apart from the odd reverted green shoots which must not be allowed to take over.

Forsythia 'Lynwood' (Golden Bell Bush)

- Deciduous shrub
- Hardiness – H1
- Care – Easy to average

Description Height and spread to about 8ft(2.5m) and more. A quick growing popular and reliable flowering shrub with stiff open bushy habit. The rich golden yellow flowers are freely produced between March and May on naked branches. The dark green leaves are useful as a backdrop for summer flowers but are otherwise rather ordinary. A good shrub for town, coast and most other situations.

Maturity Quite rapid – flowers within 2 or 3 years of planting.

Fig 70 Euonymus 'Emerald n'Gold' with its evergreen foliage makes a dense weed-smothering ground cover.

Fig 71 Forsythia, with its gleaming golden flowers puts on a bold, spectacular and reliable display in spring. Best when fully grown – it makes a medium to large shrub.

Lifespan   30 years and more.

Other varieties   *F. suspensa*. Height and spread to 10ft(3m). With its pendulous intertwining branches it makes a first class wall shrub.

Uses   Good for hedges and screens; an excellent back of border or wall shrub; suitable as an accent plant; and first class for cutting. If cut in tight bud in December, sprigs can be forced into bloom by simply standing in water at room temperature.

Planting   Set out from autumn to spring allowing a minimum 5ft(1.5m) spread.

Position   Best in a sunny open spot but adapts well to partial shade.

Soil   Unfussy and grows in most soils of reasonable fertility including those of an alkaline or clayish nature.

Propagation   Root semi-ripe node cuttings in summer under cover. Alternatively take hardwood cuttings in October or November and root under cover or in a warm sheltered spot in the open. Forsythia cuttings rarely fail.

Treatment   Keep young plants well watered when grown on light soils.

Pruning   PG1 and PG2 for unclipped shrubs. PG6 for clipped hedges. Shorten back new wood by one third at planting time to encourage bushiness. Cut out thin or flowered shoots in May on bushes, and clip hedges and formal bushes at the same time. Rejuvenate old shrubs by hard pruning in spring – about May.

Problems   Trouble free.

Garrya elliptica (Silk Tassel)

- Evergreen shrub or small tree
- Hardiness – H2–H3
- Care – Easy

Description   Height to about 10ft(3m). Spread 8ft(2.5m) in average conditions increasing by 50 per cent in very mild climates. A rapidly growing leafy shrub or small tree of bushy habit, grown largely for its foliage and winter interest. From November to February enormous silvery-grey catkins, up to 9in(23cm) in length, hang down like silken tassels – hence its popular name. The leaves are glossy dark green and leathery. Opt for male plants as they produce the longest catkins.

Maturity   Instant foliage effects. It will take up to 3 years for the catkins to appear.

Lifespan   30 years plus.

Other varieties.   *G.e.* 'James Roof'. Carries the longest catkins of any variety – up to 1ft(30cm). Male and similar to above.

Uses   Excellent as a wall shrub and as a freestanding border shrub. Popular with arrangers for cutting.

Planting   Set out young, male container grown plants in spring before they get pot-bound. Garrya resents root disturbance and is slow to re-establish if the roots are disturbed. Allow a 7ft(2m) minimum spread.

Position   Adapts to sun or partial shade. Does well even on north and east walls, if sheltered from cold winds. Shelter is very important.

Soil   Grows satisfactorily on most moist, well-drained soils of average fertility. Tolerant of alkaline and medium to heavy soils.

Propagation   Root semi-ripe heel cuttings in July or August under cover. Alternatively, peg down layers in September.

Treatment   Protect from drying winds and frost especially when young. Keep well watered for the first two years at least.

Pruning   PG5. Minimal, save shortening straggly shoots in late spring.

Problems   Frost prone in spring when young but otherwise trouble free.

Genista lydia (Broom)

- Deciduous shrub
- Hardiness – H2
- Care – Average

Description   Height about 2ft(60cm). Spread 4ft(1.2m) or more. A moderately quick growing low, free-flowering shrub with lax arching or prostrate stems. Masses of scented gold-yellow pea-like flowers smother the slender stems during

May and June. The mid-green leaves open at flowering time. Good in coastal districts.

Maturity   Flowers within 2 years of planting.

Lifespan   8–10 years.

Other varieties   *G. hispanica* (Spanish Broom). Forms a ground hugging stiff spiny mound but otherwise similar to above.

Uses   Suitable for ground cover and rock garden specimens. Excellent on banks and for trailing over walls.

Planting   Set out pot-grown plants – preferably in spring with autumn as second best. Disturb the roots as little as possible. Allow a minimum 3ft(90cm) spread.

Position   An open sunny site or warm bank is best. Avoid planting in any very exposed places.

Soil   A light, well-drained sandy soil that is not too rich helps to ensure free flowering but worth trying in any average garden soil.

Propagation   For best results take semi-ripe heel cuttings in July and root singly in small pots under cover – in this way the roots receive minimal disturbance.

Treatment   In early days take all practical steps to reduce competition from weeds and nearby plants.

Pruning   PG1. Shorten back flowered shoots immediately blooming is over to reduce seed set and the consequential exhaustion of the shrub.

Problems   Trouble free.

Hamamelis mollis (Witch Hazel)

- Deciduous shrub or small tree
- Hardiness – H2
- Care – Easy

Description   Height and spread 7ft(2m) plus. A slow to moderately quick growing choice flowering and foliage shrub. It has distinctive zigzag branch form and a spreading yet ascending habit. Crowded clusters of sweetly scented yellow and red flowers are carried on naked branches between December and March. The green summer leaves turn through delightful golden yellow autumn tints before they fall.

Maturity   Autumn tints within 12 months of setting out young plants. Flowers within 2–3 years.

Lifespan   30 years plus.

Other varieties   *H. 'Pallida'* has a shorter flowering season than above but otherwise similar in most respects. Expect yellow flowers in January and February.

Uses   Excellent as a wall shrub or free-standing specimen near doors and windows where the scent can waft inside. First class for cutting for the house.

Planting   Set out in late autumn/early winter or spring. Allow a minimum spread of 6ft(1.8m).

Position   Adapts to sun or light partial shade. Needs to be sheltered from cold drying north and east winds. Avoid situations exposed to early morning sun and the damaging consequential rapid thaw after overnight frost.

Soil   Cool, deep, well-drained light to medium loam, well supplied with organic matter suits best. Most soils of average fertility will suffice.

Propagation   Named varieties are normally grafted in April under cover onto *H. virginiana* rootstocks. Alternatively, peg down layers in September.

Treatment   Give young plants every assistance to get established. Keep them weed-free, mulched and well watered for the first few seasons.

Pruning   PG5. Minimal beyond correcting misplaced shoots in autumn.

Problems   Normally trouble free.

Hedera helix 'Goldheart' (Ivy)

- Evergreen climber
- Hardiness – H1–H2
- Care – Easy to average

Description   Height and spread 10ft(3m) plus. 'Goldheart' is one of the smaller leaved ivies, and is a highly popular and widely grown self-clinging climber. The leaves are glossy, rich green and have bright golden centres. The stems cling to nearby supports by means of aerial roots. Slow growing at first, it increases with age to moderately quick growing.

Fig 72 Hedera 'Goldheart' seen here as a garden centre plant is excellent for brightening up drab walls when trellis trained. Its gold splashed evergreen foliage is outstanding.

Maturity Instant foliage appeal.

Lifespan 20 years – up to double this figure.

Other varieties H. h. 'Buttercup'. Height and spread 8ft(2.5m). Pleasing golden yellow leaves which turn greenish yellow with age. Otherwise much the same as 'Goldheart'.

Uses Effective as a wall covering when trained upwards as a climber or allowed to hang over low walls. Good in hanging and wall baskets.

Planting Set out in mild spells between autumn and spring. Allow direct planted wall specimens at least 6ft(1.8m) of wall space.

Position Colourings are best in sun but adapts well to partial shade. Can be grown on north and east aspects as well as south and west walls.

Soil Thrives in almost any soil of average fertility including those of a clayish or alkaline nature. Peat-based mixtures are fine for short stay container plantings of up to six months – otherwise stick to soil-based composts.

Propagation Root semi-ripe node cuttings in summer under cover.

Treatment Train ivies over wall mounted trellis rather than allowing them to cling direct to the wall when the risk is damage to the masonry.

98

Pruning PG7. Little needed apart from shortening shoots back to allotted area during spring or summer.

Problems Occasionally comes under attack from scale insects but otherwise fairly trouble free.

Hibiscus syriacus 'Woodbridge'
(Tree Hollyhock)

- Deciduous shrub
- Hardiness – H2
- Care – Average

Description Height and spread to 7ft(2m) and more. A moderately quick growing spectacular flowering bush with numerous erect branches. Rich pink, carmine centred flowers are freely

Fig 73 Hibiscus – autumn colour can be relied on.

carried among the leafy green foliage during late summer and autumn.

Maturity Flowering normally begins within 1 or 2 years of planting.

Lifespan 20 years and more.

Other varieties Two excellent varieties of similar size and habit are *H.s.* 'Blue Bird' with large blue blooms and *H.s.* 'Hamabo' with crimson blotched blush white flowers.

Uses Sound choice for beds and borders and to grow as a wall shrub. Effective in containers. Useful for flower arrangers.

Planting Set out during mild spells between autumn and spring. Allow direct planted shrubs a minimum 5ft(1.5m) spread. A minimum 1ft(30cm) container is needed.

Position Needs an open but sheltered sunny spot.

Soil Thrives in almost any reasonably fertile, preferably moist, soil including those of an alkaline or heavy nature. Avoid shallow or sandy soils liable to dry out.

Propagation Semi-ripe heel cuttings taken in July root readily under cover in warmth.

Treatment Keep well watered until established.

Pruning PG3 and PG5. Prune after flowering or in early spring. In restricted spaces, cut out flowered wood back to the main framework. Where there is more room simply thin out the flowered wood.

Problems Likely to drop buds if subjected to severe drought.

Hippophae rhamnoides (Sea Buckthorn)

- Deciduous shrub
- Hardiness – H2
- Care – Easy

Description Height 15ft(4.5m). Spread 8ft(2.5m) or more. A fairly tough but nonetheless attractive, moderately quick growing, fruiting and foliage shrub for the larger garden. When young, the habit is open, spiny and sparse branching, becoming rounded and dense with age. In-significant flowers bloom in April, and on female plants they are followed by eyecatching, long lasting orange-red berries from September to February. Birds do not as a rule eat these extremely bitter fruits. The willow-lookalike leaves are silvery white in summer. Good in coastal areas being wind resistant and salt tolerant – adapts well to inland sites too.

Maturity Foliage appeal from planting time during summer. Berry colour in 2–3 years but can take longer.

Lifespan 20 years plus.

Other varieties At present there are no other garden worthy varieties of note.

Uses Makes an effective intruder resistant hedge or screen.

Planting Set out during mild spells between autumn and spring, spacing hedging plants 2ft(60cm) apart. Allow a 5ft(1.5m) spread in borders. For berrying, set out both male and female plants. One male will pollinate up to six female shrubs.

Position Needs an open sunny situation.

Soil Thrives in most soils of average fertility and flourishes in those of a dry sandy nature. Suitable for alkaline soils given reasonable drainage.

Propagation Peg down layers of both male and female plants in September. Another alternative is to sow seed in October but the sexes cannot be determined until flowering begins.

Treatment Shorten back young plants by one third at planting time to ensure bushiness.

Pruning PG5. Clip hedges and prune back straggly growths in August.

Problems Trouble free.

Hydrangea macrophylla 'Blue Wave' (Lacecap Hydrangea)

- Deciduous shrub
- Hardiness – H2
- Care – Average

Description Height and spread 6ft(1.8m) but much more in very mild climates. An outstanding, moderately quick growing, flowering shrub of domed or vaguely rounded habit and stiff twiggy branches. The flower heads are large and plate sized – an outer ring of larger florets surrounds a circle of small fertile florets. The outer ring is blue on acid soils but pink when grown on soils of a slightly alkaline nature. The large green leaves show off the flowers to advantage. First rate in coastal areas.

Maturity Provided well grown plants are set out will flower within 12 months.

Lifespan About 10 years for direct planted stock. Container plants are best replaced annually or biennially.

Other varieties *H.m.* 'White Wave'. A white flowered form of the above.

Uses Excellent in beds and borders as an accent plant or grow as a specimen. Good in containers and popular with arrangers for cutting.

Planting Set out in spring when the risk of frost damage is past. Allow a spread of about 4ft(1.2m) in beds.

Position Grows well in sun or partial shade given a sheltered position. Not a shrub for east-facing sites.

Soil Needs a deep, rich, moist cool, free-draining soil.

Propagation Root semi-ripe node cuttings in July under cover in warmth.

Treatment Keep well watered and feed occasionally during the growing season using liquid high potash fertiliser.

Pruning PG2 and PG5. Minimal – simply thin out any overcrowded, outworn and weak shoots after flowering. Dead flower heads give frost protection to next year's flower buds and so leave intact until spring. Windy gardens are the

Fig 74 Hydrangea 'Blue Wave' is a very fine summer flowering shrub for mild, sunny coastal districts.

Fig 75 Few, if any, ground cover shrubs can outshine Hypericum calcycinum. *Its versatility is outstanding.*

exception and you should dead-head in autumn to reduce wind resistance.

Problems Aphids are occasionally a nuisance. Chlorosis is a problem on highly alkaline soils.

Hypericum calcycinum (Rose of Sharon)

- Evergreen shrub
- Hardiness – HI
- Care – Easy to average

Description Height to about Ift(30cm). Spread indefinite. A moderate to quick growing low bushy flowering shrub which spreads by means of suckers. Flowering period is from June to September when the yellow flowers are set off by the green leaves. A most tolerant shrub suited to most situations including town and coast and those of a difficult nature.

Maturity Normally starts to flower within I or 2 years of planting.

Lifespan I5 years at least.

Other varieties *H. x moserianum*. Height 2ft(60cm). Spread 2½ft(75cm). Of tufted habit – semi-evergreen with red stems, yellow summer flowers and a hardiness rating of H2. Otherwise as above.

Uses Excellent as ground cover. Useful for underplanting and for stabilizing banks.

Planting Set out in autumn or spring. To obtain quick ground cover space shrubs about Ift(30cm) apart.

Position Grows well in sun or semi-shade.

Soil Adapts to most free-draining soils of average fertility ranging from dry sandy loams to heavy moist soils and including alkaline conditions.

Propagation Root semi-ripe node cuttings under cover in June and July. Division is a practical alternative – a job for autumn or spring.

Treatment Keep well watered until established.

Pruning PG3. Cut back frosted or worn out tops in late spring. Keep ageing clumps within allotted space by cutting around annually with a spade and removing surplus suckers.

Problems Occasional attacks of rust are possible. When everything is to its liking it can be invasive.

Ilex aquifolium 'Madame Briot' (Holly)

- Evergreen shrub or tree
- Hardiness – HI
- Care – Easy to average

Description Height to about 13ft(4m). Spread 10ft(3m). A large slow growing, bushy, prickly shrub or small tree grown mainly for its foliage with the added bonus of berries. The leaves are leathery, glossy, very spiny and golden variegated. The young stems are purple. 'Madame Briot' is a female variety and if pollinated carries red berries in autumn and winter.

Maturity Instant foliage appeal. Berrying 5-7 years.

Lifespan Healthy plants – upwards of 80 years.

Other varieties *I.a.* 'Argentea Marginata'. As above but with silvery white margined leaves and green stems. A free berrying female variety.

Uses Best reserved to grow as a clipped specimen shrub or hedge.

Planting Set out in autumn or spring allowing 1½ft(45cm) spacing for hedges and 5ft(1.5m) minimum spread for specimens.

Position For a profusion of berries select a partially shaded, not too exposed spot. Plant both male and female shrubs – one male to six female.

Soil Thrives on any well-drained soil of reasonable fertility including alkaline.

Propagation Root semi-ripe heel or node cuttings in June under cover.

Treatment Initially keep watered and mulched.

Pruning PG6. Clip hedges and specimens to shape in late spring or summer.

Problems Susceptible to leaf miner attack.

Jasminum nudiflorum (Winter Jasmine)

- Deciduous wall shrub
- Hardiness – HI–H2
- Care – Average

Description Height and spread to 10ft(3m) when wall trained. A popular moderate to quick growing, rambling, flowering shrub with slender stems which are best supported. A succession of primrose yellow flowers are carried on bare branches during mild spells between November and April. In summer the stems are mostly hidden by the lustrous green leaves.

Maturity Flowers within 1 or 2 years of planting.

Lifespan 10–12 years at least.

Other varieties *J. officinale* 'Grandiflorum' Height to 30ft(9m). Spread 10ft(3m). A vigorous, sweet scented, white summer flowering twining deciduous climber.

Fig 76 As a winter flowering wall shrub, Jasminum nudiflorum makes a welcome addition to any garden.

Uses   Essentially a wall shrub for training up vertical surfaces but also suitable for draping down over a retaining wall. Popular for cutting.

Planting   Set out between autumn and spring. Allow each plant a minimum 6ft(1.8m) spread.

Position   A sunny south or west wall or fence is best. It will adapt to a part-shaded north or east aspect if not too exposed. Easterly aspects unless sheltered from early morning sun are least desirable of all.

Soil   Any free-draining soil of average fertility including alkaline, will do. But avoid over rich conditions.

Propagation   Root semi-ripe heel or node cuttings in summer under cover. Alternatively peg down layers in September.

Treatment   Tie into trellis-type supports fixed to walls or fences.

Pruning   PG2. Thin out weak and flowered stems in spring as blooming finishes.

Problems   Aphids, including blackfly, can be troublesome.

Kalmia latifolia (Calico Bush)

- Evergreen shrub
- Hardiness – H2–H3
- Care – Easy

Description   Height and spread up to 10ft(3m). A slow growing, robust but choice flowering shrub of vaguely rounded, bushy habit. Beautiful clusters of rose coloured flowers appear in June – set off by rich, glossy green leaves. Best reserved for mild, moist climates. The foliage is poisonous to sheep.

Maturity   Flowering normally starts within 2–3 years of planting.

Lifespan   15 years in favourable conditions.

Other varieties   *K.l.* 'Ostbo Red' has red flowers but is otherwise similar to the above.

Uses   Makes a fine specimen shrub in lawn, bed or border. Useful in containers.

Planting   Set out in autumn or spring. Allow a minimum 6ft(1.8m) spread.

Position   Adapts to sun or light partial shade.

Fig 77   Kalmia latifolia *'Clementine Churchill' is first class on acid soils – given some shelter from cold winds.*

Needs to be sheltered from cold or drying winds, from the north or east especially.

Soil   Cool, moist and peaty acid soil. Use lime-free peat or soil-based compost in containers.

Propagation   Peg down layers in September.

Treatment   Protect newly planted shrubs from wind – vital during their first winter.

Pruning   PG5. Minimal – shorten straggly or misplaced shoots in late spring or summer.

Problems   Trouble free.

Kerria japonica 'Pleniflora' (Bachelors' Buttons)

- Deciduous shrub
- Hardiness – H1–H2
- Care – Easy to average

Description   Height 7ft(2m). Spread 6ft(1.8m). A moderate to quick growing, fairly tall, graceful flowering shrub with slender erect suckering branches. Double yellow pompon flowers are carried on bright green stems during April and May just as the shrub is leafing up. The green leaves provide a pleasing foil to the flowers. The naked stems retain their colouring during winter

Fig 78 Kerria 'Pleniflora' is a cheerful sight in spring with its orange-yellow pompons and bright green stems.

thus providing interest during the darker months.

Maturity Flowering begins within 1 or 2 years of planting.

Lifespan 10 years at least.

Other varieties *K.j.* 'Variegata'. Height and spread 3ft(90cm). Single yellow spring flowers, with creamy white variegated summer leaves — otherwise a scaled down version similar to the above.

Uses A good wall shrub; interesting in borders; and popular for cutting.

Planting Set out between autumn and spring. Allow a minimum 3ft(90cm) spread.

Position Semi-shade preferred.

Soil Does best in a moist, free-draining, medium to heavy loam of average fertility.

Propagation Semi-ripe node cuttings, taken in July or August root readily under cover.

Treatment Keep well watered after planting. And liquid feed during the first growing season to give it a good start.

Pruning PG2. Minimal — thin out weak and spindly shoots along with any outworn flowered stems in late spring after flowering has finished.

Problems Generally trouble free.

Lavandula 'Hidcote' (Lavender)

- Evergreen shrub
- Hardiness — H2
- Care — Easy to average

Description Height to 1ft(30cm). Spread 1½ft(45cm). One of the most popular and best loved cottage garden shrubs. Moderately quick growing it is noted for its fragrance, flowers and foliage. Spikes of fragrant purple flowers are carried on slender stalks to scent the air from July to September. Silvery grey aromatic foliage provides year round interest. Does well in coastal areas.

Maturity Flowers within a year of planting.

Lifespan 15 years or so.

Other varieties *L.* 'Munstead Dwarf'. Height and spread 2ft(60cm). A blue flowered variety otherwise much the same as 'Hidcote'.

Uses Excellent as edging to beds and borders. useful on hot banks and slopes. Grow near to doors and windows for fragrance. Popular for cutting.

Planting Set out in autumn or spring, spacing plants about 1ft(30cm) apart for edging.

Position Needs sun and warmth. Avoid very exposed situations.

Soil Thrives on a free-draining light to medium loam of average fertility, avoid anything too rich. Tolerant of alkaline soils.

Propagation Root semi-ripe heel or node cuttings under cover during July or August.

Treatment Keep weed-free and avoid competition in early days — slow to establish.

Pruning PG6. Clip off old flower heads in late autumn and trim over lightly in spring.

Problems Sometimes comes under attack from froghopper/spittlebug.

Ligustrum ovalifolium 'Aureum' (Golden Privet)

- Semi-evergreen shrub
- Hardiness — H1–H2
- Care — Average to above average

Description Height to 7ft(2m) or more. Spread 6ft(1.8m) and over. A highly popular, slow to quick growing, dense, bushy, much branched shrub noted for its foliage appeal. The leaves are green centred with bright gold margins. If left un-trimmed clusters of fragrant white flowers will appear between July and September. Equally at home in town, coast and country. Leaves are re-tained in mild winters but dropped during pro-longed severe weather.

Maturity Instant foliage appeal. Flowering begins in earnest in 4 or 5 years.

Lifespan 30 years or more.

Other varieties *L. ovalifolium.* Height 13ft(4m). Spread 10ft(3m). A vigorous green leaved form. Freer flowering, quicker growing and longer lived than 'Aureum'.

Uses Widely grown as hedging; a good specimen shrub both in mixed borders and con-tainers; useful for cutting.

Planting Set out in autumn or spring. Space plants 1½ft(45cm) apart for hedging. Allow a spread of at least 3ft(90cm) for specimen shrubs.

Position Grows well in sun or partial shade – preferably not too exposed.

Soil Adapts to most well-drained soils of average fertility including those of an alkaline nature.

Propagation Take hardwood node cuttings in October and either root under cover or in a warm, sheltered spot outdoors.

Treatment Keep well watered and mulched during the first summer at least.

Pruning PG6. Shorten back plants by one third after planting. Clip hedges and formal bushes at least two or three times during the growing season, starting in May. Cut out any reverted green shoots or branches on sight.

Problems Occasional reversion to green leaved form.

Lonicera periclymenum 'Belgica'
(Honeysuckle)

- Deciduous climber
- Hardiness – H1–H2
- Care – Average

Description Height to 13ft(4m). Spread 10ft(3m) and over. A quick growing twining climber noted for its supremely fragrant flowers. Sweetly scented rose-purple and creamy-yellow

Fig 79 Ligustrum ovalifolium 'Aureum' (Golden Privet) is a fine hedging plant and valuable for formal clipping or topiary work. Grows well in most soils, is good in towns and colours best in sun.

Fig 80 Honeysuckle is a popular climber with sweetly scented flowers.

flowers bloom from May to July to be followed by clusters of translucent red berries in late summer. The leaves are blue-green and unspectacular.

Maturity Flowering commences within 1 or 2 years of planting.

Lifespan 30 years or more.

Other varieties *L.p.* 'Serotina' (Late Dutch Honeysuckle). Similar to 'Belgica' in most respects but has more deeply coloured blooms and flowers from July to September.

Uses Excellent for training over pergolas, porches, arches, sheds and walls, for rambling through trees; and for cutting.

Planting Set out plants between autumn and spring. Allow a minimum 5ft(1.5m) spread.

Position Best in partial light shade, but grows well in sun, provided the roots are kept shaded and cool. Shelter is needed for optimum effect.

Soil Needs a moist, cool, leafy or humus-rich soil of average to high fertility. Tolerant of moderately alkaline soils.

Propagation Root semi-ripe node cuttings under cover in August.

Treatment Keep well watered and mulched especially in the first year after planting.

Pruning PG7. After flowering, thin out old stems and shorten back growths to keep within allotted space every 2 or 3 years.

Problems Susceptible to occasional attacks by leaf spot and/or mildew.

Magnolia × soulangiana 'Lennei' (Magnolia)

- Deciduous shrub or tree
- Hardiness – H2
- Care – Easy

Description Height 13ft(4m) or more. Spread 10ft(3m) and over. A noble shrub or small tree of basal branching, open spreading habit, slow growing in the early years but moderately quick later on. Magnolia is grown for its magnificent flowers. Individual blooms are large and bold, tulip or goblet shaped, rose-purple on the outside, creamy-white tinged pale pink-purple on

Fig 81 *Magnolia 'Lennei' with its bold, goblet-like flowers is one of gardening's gems. It makes a first-class specimen shrub.*

the inside. The flowering period is April and May. When well grown the leaves are large, lustrous and rich green.

Maturity Wait 3–5 years for flowering to begin.

Lifespan 60 years.

Other varieties *M. × s.* 'Rubra'. Height 8ft(2.5m). Spread 6ft(1.8m). The blooms are mauve-purple. In other respects similar to above.

Uses Normally grown as a specimen shrub.

Planting Set out in spring. Allow an uninterrupted minimum spread of 10ft(3m).

Position Grows well in sun or partial light shade. Needs protection from cold spring winds especially from the north and east. Shade from early morning sun to avoid a rapid thaw after spring frosts.

Soil Needs a deep, moist, fertile, rich loam acid to neutral soil.

Propagation Peg down layers in March or April. Root semi-ripe heel cuttings under cover in July.

Treatment Protect the roots of young stock with winter mulches of straw to minimize the risk of frost injury. Keep well watered and mulched during summer.

Pruning PG2 and PG5. Where space is restricted, thin out old flowered wood after flowering. Otherwise minimal pruning needed.

Problems Susceptible to spring frosts.

Mahonia aquifolium (Oregon Grape)

- Evergreen shrub
- Hardiness – HI
- Care – Easy to average

Description Height to 3ft(90cm). Spread to 4ft(I.2m). A moderately quick growing, widely grown, thicket forming, suckering shrub renowned for its flowers and bold foliage. The sweetly fragrant yellow flower spikes are usually at their best during March and April. Clusters of blue-black berries follow from midsummer to autumn. The large rich green, shiny summer leaves turn through bronze purple and red tints during autumn. Good in towns and at the coast.

Maturity Instant foliage interest. Flowering and berrying begin within 1 or 2 years of setting out.

Other varieties M. x 'Charity'. Height 7ft(2m). Spread 6ft(I.8m). Slightly less hardy than the above. The long lemon yellow flower spikes bloom at about the same time. The leaves are larger, pinnate and holly-like.

Uses Effective as ground cover and under-planting. Useful for cutting.

Fig 82 Mahonia 'Apollo' flowers freely in partial shade. This is a multi-bonus small to medium sized shrub providing scent, colour, flowers, berries and attractive evergreen holly-like foliage.

Planting Set out in spring and autumn. Allow a minimum 2½ft(75cm) spread. Plant in groups where space permits.

Position Adapts to sun or shade. Needs shelter from freezing easterly or northerly winter and spring winds.

Soil Prefers a cool, moist, peaty or leafy soil that is well-drained. Tolerant of alkaline as well as medium to heavy soils.

Propagation Root tip cuttings under cover during July and August.

Treatment Protect young plants from cold, drying winds during their first winter and make sure they are well mulched and watered during hot dry spells.

Pruning PG2. Selectively thin out weak, over-crowded, and flowered shoots after flowering in late spring, removing about a quarter of the total bush each year.

Problems Occasionally attacked by rust and mildew.

Myrtus communis (Myrtle)

- Evergreen shrub
- Hardiness – H2–H3
- Care – Easy

Description Height 10ft(3m) and more. Spread 13ft(4m) or over. A moderate to quick growing leafy, aromatic, much branched shrub grown for both flowers and foliage. Scented white flowers nestle amongst the dark glossy green leathery leaves during July and August. Inconspicuous reddish black berries follow. When crushed, the leaves are noticeably aromatic. Good in mild coastal areas.

Maturity Immediate foliage interest. Flowering normally starts within 2 or 3 years of setting out.

Lifespan 40 years and often more.

Other varieties M.c. 'Tarentina'. Height 3ft(90cm). Spread 2ft(60cm). A smaller more refined version of the above.

Uses Popular as a wall shrub as well as in mixed borders. Useful for cutting.

Planting Set out in spring. Allow a minimum

spread of 6ft(1.8m) in borders but more for wall trained plants.

Position Needs a warm, sunny situation, sheltered from cold north and east winds.

Soil Prefers a medium to light leafy, well-drained soil, of average to above average fertility.

Propagation Root semi-ripe heel or node cuttings in July at room temperature of about 65°F(16°C).

Treatment Protect from wind – vital during the first winter. Keep well watered and mulched at least until established.

Pruning PG5. Minimal – apart from an occasional trimming to shape in late spring or summer.

Problems Normally trouble free.

Olearia haastii (Daisy Bush)

- Evergreen shrub
- Hardiness – H2
- Care – Easy

Description Height 6ft(1.8m) or over. Spread 7ft(2m). A moderately quick growing, fairly tough, rounded bushy foliage and flowering shrub of considerable versatility. A profusion of white, daisy-like blooms are produced from July to September to smother the foliage. The sage green, glossy, leathery leaves have felted grey undersides and are fairly wind resistant and tolerant of sea spray drift.

Maturity Instant foliage appeal. Flowering may not begin for 3–4 years.

Lifespan 15 years upwards.

Other varieties O. macrodonta. A less hardy quicker growing shrub with fragrant white late summer flowers. The handsome large leathery leaves are bronzy-green with whitish felted undersides.

Uses Effective as hedging and screening especially in coastal areas; good in beds and mixed borders; suitable for container growing; and useful for cutting.

Planting Set out in autumn or spring. Allow 1½ft(45cm) spacing for hedging; 3ft(90cm) for

screening; or 4ft(1.2m) minimum spread in beds and borders.

Position Best in sun but adapts to light partial shade.

Soil Grows well in most free-draining soils of average fertility, including those of a lime-rich nature.

Propagation Root semi-ripe heel or node cuttings under cover in July or August.

Treatment Until young plants are established, keep them well watered and mulched during dry spells, and shelter them from cold drying winds – especially important during their first winter.

Pruning PG5 and PG6. Prune after flowering. Formally trained shrubs are clipped and semi-formal specimens are shortened back to shape.

Problems Normally trouble free.

Osmanthus delavayi (Osmanthus)

- Evergreen shrub
- Hardiness – H2
- Care – Easy

Description Height 5ft(1.5m). Spread 4ft(1.2m) or more. A highly pleasing, slow growing, finely textured, spreading rounded shrub of bushy habit and great charm noted for its flowers and foliage. Clusters of sweetly scented, white flowers appear in April amongst the glossy, dark green leaves.

Maturity Instant foliage interest. Flowering begins within 2 or 3 years.

Lifespan 25 years.

Other varieties O. x burkwoodii (Osmarea). Height and spread 7ft(2m). Although larger than above is a compact neat shrub with similar foliage and flowers.

Uses A pleasing small specimen shrub; effective in mixed plantings in beds and borders; good for cutting.

Planting Preferably set out in spring with autumn as second best alternative. Allow a minimum 3ft(90cm) spread.

Position Grow in sun or light partial shade, sheltered from freezing or drying spring winds.

Soil Any free-draining moist soil of average fertility is suitable. Tolerant of alkaline conditions.

Propagation Root semi-ripe heel or node cuttings during July or August in warmth at 65°F(18°C).

Treatment Protect from wind especially during first winter. Keep the roots moist, cool and mulched, especially during first summer.

Pruning PG5 and PG6. Minimal – apart from shortening any misplaced shoots after flowering. Stands clipping if a formal effect is required.

Problems Generally trouble free.

Pachysandra terminalis 'Variegata' (Japanese Spurge)

- Evergreen shrub
- Hardiness – H2–H3
- Care – Easy

Description Height 8in(20cm). Spread 1½ft(45cm). A slow to moderately quick growing pretty little carpeting shrub renowned mainly for foliage effect. White variegated leaves provide year round interest – tiny greenish white flowers appear from February to March.

Maturity Foliage/flower effects in first year.

Lifespan Up to 10 years.

Other varieties P. terminalis is green leaved, hardier, quicker growing and more vigorous than 'Variegata' but otherwise broadly similar.

Uses A ground cover shrub, well suited for underplanting beneath tree or shrub canopy.

Planting Preferably set out in spring with autumn as second alternative. Space plants about 1½ft(45cm) apart in groups or blocks.

Position Best in partial or light shade, preferably sheltered from strong winds.

Soil Grows in any moist, weed-free, well-drained soil of average fertility, alkaline included.

Propagation Division in March. Lift, split up and replant clumps immediately.

Treatment Keep weed-free and well watered until properly established.

Pruning PG5. Not as a rule necessary.

Problems Normally trouble free.

Parthenocissus henryana (Henry's Creeper)

- Deciduous climber
- Hardiness – H2
- Care – Easy to average

Description Height about 18ft(5m). Spread 10ft(3m). A quick growing valued, self-clinging, branching climber noted for its brilliant foliage. The leaves are dark green with silver and pink markings. In autumn the green portions turn through shades of vivid red and crimson before dropping. The summer flowers are greenish and inconspicuous. This climber attaches itself to nearby supports by means of sucker pads and tendrils.

Maturity Vivid autumn tints from the first year onwards.

Lifespan 40 years and more – given attention.

Other varieties P. tricuspidata veitchii. Height 25ft(7.5m). Spread 20ft(6m). Green summer foliage turns through unsurpassed crimson, red, scarlet and flame autumn tints.

Uses An outstanding wall covering and excellent for training over pergolas, arches, rafters and sheds.

Planting Set out anytime from autumn to spring as soil and weather permit. Allow a minimum 8ft(2.5m) spread.

Position Adapts to almost any aspect but partial shaded west walls ensure the finest autumn tints.

Soil Almost any free-draining soil of average fertility should suffice but avoid planting in anything too rich.

Propagation Root node cuttings under cover in August.

Treatment To minimize the risk of structural damage train over wall mounted trellis rather than allow to cling directly onto brickwork.

Pruning PG7. Thin out overcrowded growths in summer and at the same time shorten back at the tips to restrict to allotted space.

Problems Occasionally attacked by aphids, red spider mites and scale insects.

Passiflora caerulea (Passion Flower)

- Semi-evergreen climber
- Hardiness – H3
- Care – Average to above average

Description Height about 13ft(4m). Spread 10ft(3m) or more. A rapidly growing, self clinging climber which is noted for the beauty of its flowers from June to September. The individual blooms are large, fragrant, white marked blue. Egg-shaped orange fruits follow in hot summers. Passion flower supports itself by means of tendrils. Best reserved for mild climates.
Maturity Given good cultivations flowering and fruiting can start within 12 months.
Lifespan 10 years and more with care.
Other varieties *P.c.* 'Constance Elliot' is a charming pure white flowered form.
Uses A prestigious wall covering; good in tubs; and useful as cut flowers.
Planting Set out in May. Allow a minimum 7ft(2m) wall spread.
Position Needs a warm, sunny, south or west-facing wall sheltered from wind.
Soil A moist, well-drained, rich soil of above average fertility ensures strong growth.
Propagation Root semi-ripe heel or node cuttings under cover in July or August. Overwinter the resulting young plants in cool but frost-free conditions. Provide good light and keep barely moist.
Treatment Keep newly set out plants well

Fig 83 Passiflora caerulea is noted for its particularly distinctive flowers.

watered, fed and mulched especially in the first summer. Protect them from wind and frost during their first winter.
Pruning PG3. Shorten side growths back to the main framework in about March or early April.
Problems Occasionally infected with Mosaic virus resulting in leaf mottling and stunted growth and a need to grub out the plant.

Pernettya 'Mother of Pearl' (Pernettya)

- Evergreen shrub
- Hardiness – H1–H2
- Care – Easy

Description Height 3ft(90cm). Spread indefinite. A slow to moderately quick growing, somewhat under-rated thicket or clump forming shrub. It deserves to be more widely grown for its winter berries alone. White flowers usually bloom in late April or May, to be followed by pink berries – they colour up in late summer and persist until spring. The small, neat, glossy, dark green leaves are carried on slender, wiry stems.
Maturity Instant foliage appeal. With well grown plants expect flowering and berrying in the second year.
Lifespan 12–15 years in good conditions.
Other varieties *P.* 'Bell's Seedling' – red stems and red berries. *P.* 'Snow White' – white berries. Male non-berrying *P. mucronata* is needed to ensure berrying – one per three berrying kinds.
Uses Grown as ground cover and as underplanting. Cut the odd sprig of berries for winter decoration indoors.
Planting Set out in autumn or spring. Best in groups if space allows – each plant needs a minimum spread of 2ft(60cm).
Position Adapts to sun or light partial shade. Try to shelter from direct exposure to north and east winds.
Soil Needs a cool moist, free-draining, peaty, lime-free soil which is not too rich.
Propagation Root semi-ripe heel cuttings under cover in September.

Fig 84 Grow Pernettya mucronata *'Pink Pearl' on cool, moist acid soil and, where mature, it will provide valuable berry colour from autumn to spring.*

Treatment Keep well watered, weed-free and mulched with acid peat for the first summer or two until well established.
Pruning PG5. Minimal apart from the occasional thinning out of overcrowded thickets.
Problems Generally trouble free.

Philadelphus 'Belle Etiole' (Mock Orange)

- Deciduous shrub
- Hardiness – HI–H2
- Care - Average to above average

Descriptions Height and spread 5ft(I.5m). A moderately quick to rapidly growing popular spreading bushy shrub with arching branches. Grown for its flowers and fragrance. The sweet highly scented single white flowers with pinkish-maroon tinged centres smother the branches in June and July. The leaves are ordinary.
Maturity It takes 2 or 3 years for flowering to get into full swing.

Lifespan 20 years at least.
Other varieties P. 'Virginal'. Height IOft(3m). Spread 5ft(I.5m). Of strong growing and erect habit with double or semi-double white flowers.
Uses Good in beds and borders and as a single specimen. Popular with flower arrangers.
Planting Set out between autumn and spring allowing a minimum 5ft(I.5m) spread.
Position Adapts to both sun and partial light shade.
Soil Grows well in most free draining soils of average fertility but prefers moist medium to heavy fertile loams.
Propagation Root semi-ripe heel or node cuttings under cover in July or August.
Treatment Keep well watered and mulched, especially in the first summer after planting, so as to encourage the formation of a good basic framework of branches.
Pruning PG2. Selectively thin out old branches immediately after flowering, on a three year cycle, i.e. remove a third of the branches each year.
Problems Blackfly can be a nuisance.

Phormium 'Maori Maiden' (New Zealand Flax)

- Evergreen shrub
- Hardiness – H3
- Care – Easy

Description Height and spread to about 3ft(90cm). A moderately quick growing, unusual but increasingly popular shrub grown primarily for its foliage. But is also noteworthy for its shape and form. The cream coloured leaves are leathery, long and sword-like, with a longitudinal pink stripe up the centre. The whole plant forms a dome shaped tuft. Only to be considered in mild climates.
Maturity Instant foliage appeal.
Lifespan 8–IO years with luck.
Other varieties P. cookianum 'Bronze Baby'. Height and spread to about 2½ft(75cm). Bright coppery red foliage.

Uses Effective as accent plants in beds and borders and in tubs.

Planting Set out ideally in spring. Allow a minimum spread of 3ft(90cm) or more if possible to display to full advantage.

Position Needs warmth and shelter and full sun. Positions at the base of a south or west-facing wall are ideal.

Soil Grows best in a free-draining moist, fertile medium to heavy loam.

Propagation Lift and split up sizeable clumps in April. Replant divisions immediately.

Treatment Protect the crowns of young plants from frost during winter.

Pruning PG5. Pruning is not necessary apart from the possible removal of damaged leaves on sight.

Problems Normally trouble free.

Pieris 'Forest Flame' (Andromeda)

- Evergreen shrub
- Hardiness – H3
- Care – Easy

Description Height 6ft(1.8m). Spread 5ft(1.5m). A choice, often spectacular, slow to moderately quick growing foliage and flowering shrub of rounded bushy habit with foliage almost to soil level. Clusters of pendulous white May flowers contrast with the bright red young foliage. The glossy red young leaves gradually change through pink shades to creamy white before turning green in summer. Best reserved for mild climates.

Maturity Young leaves colour up in the first spring. Flowering starts within 2 or 3 years.

Lifespan 20 years and more.

Other varieties *P. floribunda*. Height 4ft(1.2m). Spread 5ft(1.5m). Hardier than 'Forest Flame'. Lustrous rich green foliage and a very generous display of lily of the valley-like white flowers during March and April.

Uses Effective in beds and borders and for underplanting.

Planting Preferably set out in spring. Allow a 4ft(1.2m) spread.

Fig 85 Pieris is an excellent foliage shrub.

Position Needs a partially, or light dappled shaded spot with shelter from cold north and east winds.

Soil Requires a moist, free-draining, peaty or leafy acid soil that is not too rich.

Propagation Peg sown layers in September. Alternatively, root semi-ripe heel or node cuttings under cover in August.

Treatment Protect roots from frost and afford shelter from cold winds during first winter. Keep well watered and mulched in first growing season. Subsequently, mulch with peat each spring.

Pruning PG5. Little pruning is needed apart from shortening straggly or weak growths in late spring.

Problems Trouble free but likely to succumb to chlorosis if grown on alkaline soils.

Pittosporum tenuifolium (Pittosporum)   ✓

- Evergreen shrub
- Hardiness – H2–H3
- Care – Easy to average

Description Height 10ft(3m) or more. Spread 6ft(1.8m) but only in very mild areas. Is much smaller in cooler locations. A fairly slow growing dense, twiggy bush beloved by florists and flower arrangers for its distinctive foliage. The sought after shiny, pale green, wavy-edged leaves are carried on dark brown shoots. Small, insignificant, but sweet scented purple May flowers appear on mature plants.

Maturity Although foliage appeal is instant expect to wait 2–3 years before ready for cutting and for flowering to begin.

Lifespan 20 years plus.

Other varieties *P.t.* 'Garnettii'. Height 10ft(3m). Spread 4ft(1.2m). Columnar in habit with white margined grey-green leaves.

Uses Good in beds and mixed borders, and for cutting, effective as hedging, but only in very mild coastal areas.

Planting Set out in spring. Allow a spacing of 1½ft(45cm) for hedging or a 4ft(1.2m) spread for individual shrubs.

Position Adapts to sun or light shade. Must have shelter from cold north or east winds.

Soil Does best on light, well-drained leafy soil which is not too rich. Tolerates alkaline soils.

Propagation Root semi-ripe heel or node cuttings under cover in July.

Treatment Provide additional temporary wind and frost shelter during first winter after planting.

Pruning PG2 and PG6. Bush forms need occasional thinning out in late spring or summer. Trim hedges in May and September.

Problems Relatively trouble free.

Potentilla fruticosa 'Jackman's Variety' (Shrubby Cinquefoil)

- Deciduous shrub
- Hardiness – H2
- Care – Easy to average

Description Height and spread 4ft(1.2m). A moderate to quick growing, highly popular, dense bushy, rounded shrub with a long flowering season. The shrub is literally smothered with a succession of bright yellow flowers from late June to September. Bluish green leaves are carried on wiry twigs.

Fig 86 The yellow flowered potentilla contrasts well with the purple foliage behind.

Maturity Flowering begins within 12 months of planting.

Lifespan 25 years.

Other varieties *P.f.* 'Red Ace'. Height 2½ft(75cm). Spread 3½ft(1m). Vermilion-flame flowered variety.

Uses Versatile and effective in beds and mixed borders; a good specimen shrub; suitable for informal hedging; valuable in the rock garden and for container growing; useful for cutting.

Planting Set out between autumn and spring. Allow a generous 4ft(1.2m) spread for individual shrubs and 2ft(60cm) between plants for hedging. Avoid overcrowding.

Position Best in full sun but tolerant of some partial shade.

Soil Thrives in light to medium well-drained soil which is not too rich.

Propagation Root semi-ripe heel cuttings under cover in September.

Treatment Keep well watered until established.

Pruning PG2, PG5 and PG6. Clip over young plants each spring. Larger bushes are lightly trimmed in autumn.

Problems Generally trouble free.

Prunus triloba (Ornamental Almond)

- Deciduous shrub
- Hardiness – H2–H3
- Care – Average to above average

Description Height and spread 6ft(1.8m) as a free-standing shrub and increases by half as much again when grown as a wall shrub. A moderate to quick growing broad, spreading flowering shrub with stiffly ascending branches. Covered with masses of pink flowers during March and April. The leaves are green and ordinary. Best reserved for mild climates.

Maturity Flowering begins within 1 to 2 years.

Lifespan 15 years.

Other varieties P. x cistena 'Crimson Dwarf'. Height and spread 4ft(1.2m). A flowering and foliage shrub with white April flowers. Leaves open as crimson and turn through bronze-crimson to yellow in autumn before dropping. Effective hedging shrub.

Uses Best grown as a wall shrub. Effective also in containers.

Planting Set out from autumn to spring. Allow wall plants a minimum 7ft(2m) spread.

Position Ideally needs a warm sunny, sheltered south or west wall.

Soil Does well on medium, moist, free-draining reasonably rich loam. Suited to alkaline soils.

Propagation Sow seed in October under cover. Alternatively remove suckers in autumn.

Treatment Container-grown shrubs must have their roots protected from frost.

Pruning PG1. Remove all flowered stems as blooms fade in April.

Problems Occasionally attacked by aphids including blackfly.

Pyracantha 'Orange Glow' (Firethorn)

- Evergreen shrub
- Hardiness – H1–H2
- Average to above average

Fig 87 Pyracantha 'Orange Glow' is a first-class large, versatile, evergreen shrub and is suitable for use as a specimen, or for wall covering or hedging.

Description Height 13ft(4m). Spread 10ft(3m). Moderate to quick growing this is one of the best berrying shrubs. It has a dense, vigorous, free-branching habit of growth. The white hawthorn-like scented June flowers are followed by orange-red berries in autumn persisting well into winter. The leaves are glossy and dark green. Resistant to scab disease.

Maturity Flowering and berrying start in about the second year.

Lifespan 30 years.

Other varieties P. rogersiana. A red berried variety of dense erect habit.

Uses Effective as a wall shrub; good in beds and borders; makes an excellent specimen; and valued for intruder proof hedging.

Planting Set out in autumn or spring. Allow at least 7ft(2m) spread for wall and border shrubs; space hedging plants 1½ft(45cm) apart.

Position Best in partial light shade but adapts to sun in beds and borders.

Soil Prefers a moist, well-drained, fairly rich loam.

Propagation Root semi-ripe heel or node cuttings under cover in July or August.

Treatment Keep well watered and mulched during the first summer at least.

Pruning PG2 and PG6. Trim wall shrubs in May and July. Deal with free-standing bushes in July, thinning out old worn out stems.

Problems Liable to aphid attack and may succumb to fireblight disease.

Rhododendron yakushimanum 'Pink Cloud' (Rhododendron)

- Evergreen shrub
- Hardiness – HI
- Care – Easy

Description Height and spread to about 4ft(1.2m). An attractive, slow to moderately quick growing, neat and compact flowering shrub of domed shape. The large pink May and June flower clusters are effective and eyecatching. The foliage is glossy and rich dark green.

Maturity Foliage is pleasing immediately. Takes 2 or 3 years for flowering to begin.

Lifespan 20 years plus.

Other varieties R. y. 'Sparkler' – a bright red flowered form.

Uses A fine specimen or tub shrub and is effective in beds and borders too.

Planting Set out in autumn or spring. Allow a minimum 4ft(1.2m) spread.

Position Does best in dappled light or partial shade but adapts to sun. Needs shelter from strong wind.

Fig 88 Acid soil and semi-shade are necessary for the small to medium sized border shrub Rhododendron yakushimanum.

Soil Needs a moist, lime-free, peaty or leafy, not too rich free-draining soil.

Propagation Peg down layers in September. Alternatively graft indoors in April onto seedling rootstocks of R. yakushimanum. To raise rootstocks sow in February under cover.

Treatment Keep well watered when young and apply an annual peat mulch in spring.

Pruning PG5. Minimal apart from shortening the odd growth to shape in late spring and deadheading young plants taking care not to remove the following year's flower buds.

Problems Chlorosis is likely if grown on alkaline soils.

Ribes sanguineum 'Pulborough Scarlet' (Flowering Currant)

- Deciduous shrub
- Hardiness – HI
- Care – Easy to average

Description Height 8ft(2.5m). Spread 5ft(1.5m) or more. A quick growing, much loved, familiar flowering shrub with an erect open habit when

Fig 89 Ribes sanguineum is a useful medium sized shrub for hedging and mixed borders. Here it is pleasingly contrasted with golden doronicum.

young, becoming more dense with age. Clusters of pendulous red flowers adorn the naked branches in April and May as the leaves open. Clusters of black currant-like berries follow.

Maturity   Flowering and fruiting start within 1 or 2 years.

Lifespan   15 years at least.

Other varieties   *R. s.* 'Brocklebankii'. Height and spread to 4ft(1.2m). Of bushy, rounded habit with pink flowers and golden yellow foliage. Needs partial shade.

Uses   Effective in beds and mixed borders and as hedging. Good in containers and for cutting.

Planting   Set out between autumn and spring. Allow individual shrubs at least a 4ft(1.2m) spread and space hedging shrubs 2ft(60cm) apart.

Position   Best in partial or light shade but adapts well to full sun in northern gardens.

Soil   Thrives in moist, free-draining, medium to heavy, fairly rich soils of average to above average fertility. Alkaline tolerant.

Propagation   Root hardwood node cuttings under cover in autumn, alternatively root them outdoors in a warm, sheltered, well drained spot.

Treatment   Keep well watered and mulched for the first year or so.

Pruning   PG2 and PG6. Clip hedges in May or June. Also deal with bushes in May and June – tip back new growths and selectively thin out old wood in alternate years.

Problems   Trouble free.

Robinia hispida 'Rosea' (Rose Acacia)

- Deciduous shrub
- Hardiness – H2–H3
- Care – Easy to Average

Description   Height and spread to about 8ft(2.5m). An uncommon, quick growing, flowering shrub of sparsely branching habit. Pea-shaped pink flowers open during May and June. The pinnate green leaves are rather attractive.

Maturity   Normally flowers within 2–3 years.

Lifespan   15 years.

Other varieties   *R. kelseyi*. Height and spread 10ft(3m) and over. Pink flowers and bronze pinnate leaves – makes a good specimen shrub being hardier than 'Rosea'.

Uses   As a wall shrub.

Planting   Set out in autumn or spring. Allow a minimum 7ft(2m) spread.

Position   Needs full sun, plus the shelter of a south or west-facing wall.

Soil   Thrives in a light to medium, well-drained, not too rich loam of average fertility. Tolerates alkaline soils.

Propagation   Can be increased from suckers lifted in autumn. But is best raised by grafting indoors in April onto seedling rootstocks of *Robinia pseudoacacia*. Sow the seed in spring to raise the rootstocks.

Treatment   Support shrubs and tie them in.

Pruning   PG2. Selectively thin out old branches annually after flowering.

Problems   Occasional branch breakages due to storm damage, high winds or neglecting to tie in for support.

Rosmarinus officinalis (Rosemary)

- Evergreen shrub
- Hardiness – H2–H3   ✓
- Care – Average

Description   Height and spread up to 6ft(1.8m). A popular, moderately quick growing, bushy dense, aromatic shrub grown both for flower and foliage. Masses of small blue flowers smother the foliage during April and May and are then produced intermittently during summer. The needle-like leaves are green with white reverse and aromatic – most pronounced when crushed.

Maturity   Instant foliage appeal. Flowering commences in the first year, but it takes a couple of seasons to make an appreciable impact.

Lifespan   10 years if not neglected.

Other varieties   *R. o.* 'Miss Jessop's Variety'. Height 6ft(1.8m). Spread 4ft(1.2m). has a more erect, narrower habit of growth than *R. officinalis*.

Fig 90 *Rosmarinus, with its blue flowers and aromatic evergreen foliage, is a valuable garden shrub – and a popular herb too. It enjoys sun and good drainage.*

Fig 91 *The low growing* Ruta *'Jackman's Blue' with its golden flowers and blue green leaves puts on a brilliant display when grown in sun.*

Uses Most effective as formal clipped edging and hedging; it is a good specimen shrub and is useful in beds; though it is frequently grown as a culinary herb.

Planting Preferably set out in spring with autumn as second best alternative. Space hedging shrubs at least 1½ft(45cm) apart. Allow individual shrubs a minimum 3ft(90cm) spread all round.

Position Needs a warm, sunny situation, sheltered from strong winds. A south or west aspect is ideal.

Soil Generally rosemary prefers a well-drained, light to medium soil of average but not over-rich fertility.

Propagation Root semi-ripe heel or node cuttings under cover in July. Alternatively take hardwood cuttings in September and root under cover.

Treatment Keep newly set out plants weed-free and do not allow them to dry out during the first summer.

Pruning PG1 and PG6. Pinch or clip young plants two or three times during the growing season to make them bush. Trim established bushes and hedges in April.

Problems Normally trouble free.

Ruta graveolens 'Jackman's Blue' (Rue)

- Semi-evergreen or deciduous shrub
- Hardiness – H2–H3
- Care – Easy to average

Description Height to about 2ft(60cm). Spread 2½ft(75cm). A moderately quick growing dense, compact, leafy, small shrub with semi-woody stems. Grown for foliage and flower effects. Bright yellow June and July flowers contrast well against the glaucous blue filigree of foliage.

Maturity Foliage attractive right away. Flowering may be delayed until the second year.

Lifespan Best renewed every 5–7 years.

Other varieties *R. g.* 'Variegata'. A silver variegated form – not easy to obtain.

Uses Popular as edging and ground cover and as a culinary herb.

Planting Set out in autumn or spring, spacing plants about 1½ft(45cm) apart.

Position Best in a warm, sunny situation but adapts to partial shade if warm and sheltered.

Soil Grows in any well-drained, light to medium soil, of average richness and fertility.

Propagation   Root semi-ripe heel or node cuttings under cover in August.
Treatment   Keep watered during the first summer.
Pruning   PG3. Trim back all old shoots each year in April to encourage new growth.
Problems   Normally trouble free.

Salvia officinalis 'Purpurascens'
(Ornamental Sage)

- Evergreen shrub
- Hardiness – H2–H3
- Care – Easy to average

Description   Height 2ft(60cm). Spread 2½ft(75cm). A low, moderately quick growing bushy shrub which is grown mainly for its aromatic foliage. The leathery aromatic leaves and stems are green and strongly suffused with purple giving year round interest. The fragrant reddish purple flowers of June and July will last most of the summer.
Maturity   Instant foliage appeal. Often flowers in the first summer.
Lifespan   Best renewed every 5–7 years.
Other varieties   *S. o.* 'Icterina'. Grey green leaves are variegated with yellow markings.
Uses   Little grown except in collections of scented plants. It makes an effective edging and is useful for ground cover as well as a front of border plant.
Planting   Preferably set out in spring, spacing plants at least 1ft(30cm) apart.
Position   Does best in full sun, in a warm sheltered spot protected from cold winds.
Soil   Prefers a light, well-drained, not too rich loam of average fertility. Thrives in lime-rich soils.
Propagation   Root heel or node cuttings under cover in spring or September.
Treatment   Keep weed-free and prevent encroachment by other plants.
Pruning   PG2. Thin out weak or worn out growths each spring.
Problems   Subject to attack by red spider mite and leaf hopper.

Sambucus racemosus 'Sutherland'
(Golden Elder)

- Deciduous shrub
- Hardiness – H2–H3
- Care – Average to above average

Description   Height 8ft(2.5m). Spread 5ft(1.5m). One of the very best foliage and fruiting shrubs. Moderately quick growing, it has an open, spreading habit. However, it can be kept fairly compact by careful pruning. Conical clusters of white flowers open during April. Bright red berries follow in June and July. Bold deeply serrated golden leaves provide summer long colour and interest.
Maturity   Foliage interest in first year. Flowering and fruiting in third year.
Lifespan   25 years plus.
Other varieties   *S. r.* 'Plumosa Aurea'. Very similar to 'Sutherland' but the flowers are more yellowish and the leaves open bronze to turn yellow during summer.
Uses   A first-rate specimen focal point and good as an accent plant in beds and borders. Also popular for cutting.
Planting   Set out from autumn to spring. Display

Fig 92 Sambucus 'Sutherland' ultimately makes a large yellow-leaved shrub. At its best when given shelter and light shade.

to advantage by allowing a generous 6ft(1.8m) spread.

Position Does well in sun or light partial shade. Needs a sheltered spot protected from strong, drying winds.

Soil Unfussy – any free-draining soil of average fertility will do. However, it does particularly well on cool, moist, heavy, well-drained rich soils.

Propagation Root hardwood heel or node cuttings in October or November either under cover or in a warm, sheltered spot outdoors.

Treatment Stake and tie tall plants until established. Keep well watered and mulched during first summer.

Pruning PG2 and PG3. For maximum foliage effects, prune hard back to within 4in(10cm) of the ground in late autumn or winter – this is at the expense of flowers and fruits. Alternatively, for flower, berry and foliage effect prune on a three year cycle – cutting a third of the stems to near ground level each year. Expect the shrubs to grow taller.

Problems Aphids can be troublesome.

Santolina chamaecyparissus
(Cotton Lavender)

- Evergreen shrub
- Hardiness – H1–H2
- Care – Easy to average

Description Height 1½ft(45cm). Spread 2½ft(75cm). A moderate to quick growing small, compact and much branched shrub grown primarily for its foliage. The effect is dainty – composed of numerous, closely packed, silvery leaves on white woolly stems. The button-like, bright yellow flowers will be carried above the foliage from June until autumn unless prevented. The flowers tend to weaken the shrub and make it untidy.

Maturity Immediate foliage appeal. Flowering will start in the second year.

Lifespan Renew after about 7 years when shrubs become untidy.

Other varieties *S. c.* 'Nana'. Height 1ft(30cm).

Spread 1½ft(45cm). Very similar but more dense and compact.

Uses Effective for low growing hedging, edging and front of border planting. Good in rock gardens and containers.

Planting Set out in autumn or spring. Space hedging, edging and border plants about 1½ft(45cm) apart. Increase to a 2–2½ft(60–75cm) spread for single specimen plants in for example, a rock garden. Use 5in(13cm) pots for plunge planting.

Position Prefers an open, sunny situation, but adapts to partial light shade.

Soil Any free-draining soil of light to medium texture and average fertility is fine, including alkaline rich soil.

Propagation Root semi-ripe heel or node cuttings under cover in July.

Treatment Keep weed-free and well watered until established. Subsequently, keep any encroaching nearby plants in check.

Pruning PG3 and PG6. For foliage effects clip over plants in spring. Hedging and edging need a second cut about July to keep them tidy.

Problems Trouble free.

Senecio 'Sunshine' (Shrubby or Grey-leaved Senecio)

- Evergreen shrub
- Hardiness – H2–H3
- Care – Easy to average

Description Height 3ft(90cm). Spread 5ft(1.5m) or more. A moderately quick growing, dense, broad, bushy mound or dome-shaped foliage shrub. The leaves are silver-grey in the early days becoming grey-green with white felted undersides with age. Expect yellow daisy-like flowers on mature shrubs from June to August.

Maturity Instant foliage effect with flowering in the second year.

Lifespan Variable – 10 years is a good average.

Other varieties *S. monroi*. Height 5ft(1.5m). Spread 3ft(90cm). Similar to 'Sunshine' but has distinctive wavy edged leaves.

Fig 93   Senecio 'Sunshine' is a useful small evergreen shrub for seaside and sun.

Uses   Good as low hedging, especially in mild, coastal districts. Looks well with contrasting red-foliaged barberry in mixed borders.

Planting   Set out in autumn or spring. Space hedging plants 1½ft(45cm) apart. Allow single shrubs a 4ft(1.2m) spread.

Position   A sunny, open situation is best but will adapt to partial light shade. Needs protection from freezing cold winds.

Soil   Almost any medium to light, well-drained soil is suitable including those of an alkaline nature.

Propagation   Root semi-ripe heel or node cuttings under cover in July or August.

Treatment   Protect from wind and frost during the first winter.

Pruning   PG5. Minimal beyond shortening straggly or damaged shoots in May, and removing old flower clusters after blooming in autumn to avoid the nuisance of blowing seeds.

Problems   Trouble free.

Skimmia japonica 'Rubella'
(Skimmia)

- Evergreen shrub
- Hardiness – H1–H2
- Care – Easy

Description   Height 5ft(1.5m). Spread 4ft(1.2m) or more. A slow growing, naturally neat, rounded flowering shrub well covered with foliage from ground level upwards. During March, masses of red buds create a glowing haze. They then open during late March and April to expose sweetly scented pink flowers. This is a male non-berrying variety. The medium sized leaves are dark green and glossy.

Maturity   Instant foliage appeal. Flowering may not start for 3–4 years.

Lifespan   20–25 years in favourable conditions.

Other varieties   S. j. 'Foremanii'. A female variety with brilliant red berries in winter and spring. The flowers are pale and fairly inconspicuous.

Uses   Valuable for underplanting in beds and borders.

Planting   Set out in autumn or spring. Allow a minimum 4ft(1.2m) spread. Where berries are required plant 2–3 female 'Foremanii' to every male 'Rubella'.

Position   Ideally needs light or dappled shade but can adapt to afternoon sun in west-facing aspects. Shelter from north and east winds is required.

Fig 94   Skimmia japonica is invaluable for winter berry colour in towns. Plant at least one male to every four female plants to ensure pollination and fruiting.

Soil Does best in a moist, peaty, free-draining acid to neutral soil but can be grown in most soils of average fertility.

Propagation Root semi-ripe heel cuttings under cover in July or August.

Treatment Protect newly set out shrubs from wind and frost especially during their first winter.

Pruning PG5. Normally unnecessary but if thinning out is required, prune after flowering in late April or May.

Problems Trouble free.

Spiraea × bumalda 'Anthony Waterer' (Spiraea)

- Deciduous shrub
- Hardiness – HI–H2
- Care – Average

Description Height 3ft(90cm). Spread 4ft(1.2m). A low, quick growing, twiggy, thicket-forming flowering and foliage shrub. The flat clusters of carmine flowers are a feature from July to September. The leaves are light green with pink and cream variegations.

Maturity Neither flowers nor foliage make an appreciable impact until the second year.

Lifespan 15 years.

Other varieties *S. × b.* 'Goldflame'. Height and spread about 3ft(90cm). Crimson flower heads. The young leaves open gold and flame and pale towards the end of the season.

Uses Versatile, looks good in beds and borders; or as hedging and underplanting; and in tubs as well as being popular for cutting.

Planting Set out during autumn or spring. Space hedging about 2ft(60cm) apart. Allow border shrubs a minimum 3ft(90cm) spread.

Position Adapts to sun or partial light shade. Prefers not to be too exposed.

Soil Grows well in most free-draining soils of average fertility including those of an alkaline nature.

Propagation Root semi-ripe node cuttings under cover in July or August. Alternatively remove rooted divisions in October.

Fig 95 This spiraea is a memorable sight in summer when it carries carmine flowers midst its golden-green foliage.

Treatment Keep weed-free, well watered and mulched during the first year.

Pruning PG3. Cut down to almost soil level each spring.

Problems Normally trouble free.

Stranvaesia davidiana (Stranvaesia)

- Evergreen shrub or tree
- Hardiness – H2–H3
- Care – Easy to average

Description Height 13ft(4m). Spread 10ft(3m). A slow to moderately quick growing bushy, multi-purpose shrub or small tree. Grown mainly for the beauty of its berries with the added bonus of flowers and foliage. Clusters of white June flowers are followed by cotoneaster-like red berries which colour up in August and persist well into winter. The leaves are leathery – reddish in spring, turning green for the summer, then back to reddish shades again in autumn.

Maturity Although the foliage interest is immediate it is modest in the early years. Flowering and berrying may take 3–4 years.

Lifespan 25 years plus.
Other varieties *S. d.* 'Prostrata'. Height about 2ft(60cm). Spread 6ft(1.8m). A low, slow growing spreading form.
Uses Specimens make good focal points. Useful accent shrubs in beds and borders.
Planting Set out in autumn or spring. Allow a minimum 8ft(2.5m) spread.
Position Best in a sunny, not too exposed situation. Adapts to light partial shade.
Soil Grows well in almost any free-draining soil of reasonable fertility which is not too alkaline. Prefers a medium to heavy loam.
Propagation Root semi-ripe heel cuttings under cover in July or August. Alternatively sow seed in October under cover.
Treatment Protect from wind and frost during the first winter. Keep well watered and mulched during the first growing season.
Pruning PG5. Minimal – shorten straggly shoots after flowering.
Problems Fireblight attack is a potential hazard.

Symphoricarpos rivularis (S. laevigatus) (Snowberry)

- Deciduous shrub
- Hardiness – H1–H2
- Care – Average

Description Height 6ft(1.8m). Spread 5ft(1.5m). A familiar, moderate to fast growing, thicket-forming, berrying shrub with erect suckering branches. The insignificant small pink flowers of June and July are followed by clusters of marble-sized white berries in October. They persist well into winter. The leaves are green and ordinary.
Maturity Berrying normally starts within 2 or 3 years.
Lifespan 15 years plus.
Other varieties *S. chenaultii* 'Hançock'. Height 2ft(60cm). Spread 8ft(2.5m). A low growing suckering shrub with pink-purple berries.
Uses Good for underplanting and for hedges, to set in beds and borders, as well as for cutting.
Planting Set out during autumn or spring. Allow minimum 2ft(60cm) spacing for hedging. Increase this to a 4ft(1.2m) spread for border shrubs.
Position Thrives in partial or dappled shade. Tolerates some sun if not too intense.
Soil Any moist soil of average fertility will suffice.
Propagation Take hardwood cuttings in October and root outdoors in a warm, sheltered spot, or lift rooted suckers in October.
Treatment Keep well watered and mulched during the first spring and summer.
Pruning PG2 and PG6. Selectively thin out any weak and outworn stems of border shrubs in autumn and winter. Trim hedges two or three times during summer.
Problems Normally trouble free.

Syringa velutina (S. palibiniana) (Lilac)

- Deciduous shrub
- Hardiness – H2
- Care – Easy

Description Height 5ft(1.5m). Spread 4ft(1.2m) or more. A slow growing, compact, rounded twiggy flowering shrub of bushy habit. Showy clusters of small, lavender pink May flowers are freely produced. The leaves are green and provide a pleasing foil for the flowers.
Maturity Flowering begins within 3 or 4 years.

Fig 96 Symphoricarpos makes a useful shade-tolerant, background shrub for summer effect – even when not carrying its berries.

Fig 97 *Syringa (lilac) is noted for its scent as well as its flower spikes. It may be rather large for small gardens.*

Lifespan 20 years.
Other varieties *S. microphylla* 'Superba'. Height 6ft(1.8m). Spread 4ft(1.2m). Very distinctive with small green leaves, slender spreading branches and clusters of lilac-mauve June flowers, often with a second flush in September.
Uses Ideal in beds and borders or direct planted on the patio – grow in tubs in confined spaces.
Planting Set out from autumn to spring. Allow a minimum spread of 4ft(1.2m).
Position Does best in a sunny, open situation sheltered from strong winds. Adapts well to a partially shaded, west-facing aspect.
Soil Grows well in most free-draining moist soils of average fertility, including an alkaline one.
Propagation Take heel cuttings during July or August and root under cover. Graft onto privet rootstocks, under cover, during April.
Treatment Protect from wind, especially during first winter. Keep well watered during first summer.
Pruning PG5. Dead-head young plants. Shorten back any frosted tips in spring. Remove suckers on sight. Thin out weak shoots and worn out old stems.
Problems Leaf miners occasionally attack. Frost damage is possible after hard winters.

Tamarix pentandra 'Pink Cascade'
(Tamarisk)

- Deciduous shrub or small tree
- Hardiness – H2
- Care – Average to above average

Description Height 13ft(4m). Spread 8ft(2.5m) and more. A first-rate fast growing flowering shrub or small tree with long slender, willowy branches and attractive foliage. Long sprays of scented pink flowers are carried at the tips of new wood in August or early September. The feathery foliage is glaucous-blue to silvery grey.
Maturity Flowers and foliage are a feature from the first growing season.
Lifespan 15 years plus.
Other varieties *T. p.* 'Rubra' – a rose-red flowered form.
Uses Grow as a single specimen or in groups where space permits. Makes an effective hedge. Good in coastal areas.

Fig 98 *Tamarisk has very attractive feathery foliage.*

Planting Set out from autumn to spring. Space hedging shrubs 2ft(60cm) apart. Allow single specimens a minimum 8ft(2.5m) spread – reduce this to 6ft(1.8m) when planting in groups.

Position Best in full sun but adapts to partial light shade.

Soil Although tamarisk thrives in most well-drained soils of average fertility, including those of an alkaline nature, it prefers moist medium to heavy well-drained loams.

Propagation Hardwood heel or node cuttings, taken in late autumn, root readily in a sheltered warm spot outdoors.

Treatment Support young plants until established and keep well watered during first summer.

Pruning PG3. For the best flower and foliage effects, and to keep shrubs more compact, cut new growths back to within 2 buds of old wood in late autumn.

Problems Generally trouble free.

Viburnum tinus (Laurustinus)

- Evergreen shrub
- Hardiness – H2
- Care – Easy

Description Height 10ft(3m). Spread 7ft(2m) or more. A moderately quick growing dense, bushy, much branched shrub noted for its flowers and leafy foliage. Pink buds open out into white flowers over a long season from November to March. Indigo-blue berries, which later turn black, are produced rather spasmodically. A luxuriant canopy of glossy, dark green leaves.

Maturity Instant foliage appeal but it takes 3–5 years for flowering to get underway.

Lifespan 25 years and over.

Other varieties *V. t.* 'Eve Price'. Height 8ft(2.5m). Spread 5ft(1.5m). Of compact habit with rose pink buds opening to reveal pink and white flowers.

Uses A handsome specimen. Good as hedging and screening and for container growing. Popular for cutting.

Fig 99 Viburnum davidii *makes a good evergreen ground cover shrub for light shade.*

Planting Set out plants in autumn or spring. Allow a spacing of 2½ft(75cm) between plants for hedging, increase to 4ft(1.2m) for screening. Give specimens a minimum 7ft(2m) spread all round.

Position Flowers more freely in a sunny situation but grows quite happily in partial light shade.

Soil Grows well in most moist free-draining soils of average fertility including those of an alkaline nature.

Propagation Root semi-ripe heel cuttings under cover in July or August. Alternatively peg down layers in September.

Treatment Protect from wind during the first winter. Keep well watered and give the occasional high potash liquid feed during the first spring and early summer.

Pruning PG2 and PG5. Thin out weak growths and overcrowded old stems annually in spring if necessary. Minimal or no pruning is the norm on young plants.

Problems Normally trouble free.

Vinca minor 'Variegata' (Periwinkle)

- Evergreen trailing shrub
- Hardiness – HI–H2
- Care – Easy to average

Description Height 4in(10cm). Spread to 3ft(90cm). A low, slow to moderately quick growing, mat-forming, prostrate shrub. Grown for its foliage in the main, with the added bonus of flowers. The cream-variegated leaves are carried on self-rooting runners. Pale mauve-blue flowers bloom freely from March to May, then gradually tail off until about July when flowering ceases for the season.

Maturity It normally takes 2–3 years to make any appreciable impact.

Lifespan 25 years or more if not neglected.

Other varieties *V. m.* 'Bowles Variety'. Tends to be more clump forming than 'Variegata'. A plain green leaved form with blue flowers from July to October.

Uses Essentially a ground cover shrub, both in the open and for underplanting in semi-shade.

Planting Set out pot-grown plants in autumn or spring, spacing them about 1ft(30cm) apart to ensure ground cover reasonably quickly.

Position Grows in sun or shade but in very sunny situations partial light shade is advised.

Soil Does best in a cool, moist loam but grows reasonably well in most soils of average fertility including those of an alkaline nature.

Propagation Root stem cuttings in pots under cover in March or September. Alternatively increase by division in September.

Treatment Keep absolutely weed-free and well watered until a weed-proof mat is formed.

Pruning PG5 and PG7. Little pruning is needed apart from an occasional clip over in spring – a harder cut back may be needed from time to time to confine to allotted space.

Problems Normally trouble free.

Weigela florida 'Variegata' (Weigela)

- Deciduous shrub
- Hardiness – H2–H3
- Care – Easy to average

Description Height 5ft(1.5m). Spread 4ft(1.2m). A slow growing, fairly dense, bushy shrub of spreading habit, noted for its colourful foliage. The creamy-yellow variegated green leaves ensure summer long colour and interest. Numerous attractive foxglove-shaped pink flowers enliven the shrub in May and June.

Maturity Allow 2–3 years for shrubs to make any appreciable impact although flowering and foliage interest start at an early age.

Lifespan 20 years – then rapidly declines.

Other varieties *W.f.* 'Foliis Purpureis'. Height and spread about 4ft(1.2m). A dark purple foliaged form with rose-pink flowers.

Uses A valuable bed and border shrub. Good for container growing. Useful for cutting.

Planting Set out in autumn or spring. Give a minimum 4ft(1.2m) spread.

Position Adapts to sun as well as to shaded sites. Avoid exposed positions.

Soil Unfussy – grows on almost any soil of average fertility, including those of an alkaline nature.

Propagation Root semi-ripe heel or node cuttings under cover in July. Alternatively take hardwood node cuttings in October and root under cover or in a sheltered warm spot outdoors.

Treatment Keep weed-free and well watered for the first year or two after planting.

Pruning PG2 and PG3. Thin out old spent shoots in autumn. But for maximum foliage effect, cut out all but the current season's growths.

Problems Normally trouble free.

Wisteria sinensis (Wisteria)

- Deciduous climber
- Hardiness – H2–H3
- Care – Above average

Description Height 20ft(6m) and more. Spread 30ft(9m) and over. Moderate to fast growing, this is one of the most popular, twining climbers. Grown for its superb floral displays. During May and June, long pendulous racemes of sweetly scented lilac-mauve flowers grace well-grown mature plants. The long, pale green, pinnate leaves add elegance to this choice climber.

Fig 100 *Foliage shrubs like this* Weigela florida *'Variegata' have a long season of interest – with the added bonus of flowers. .*

Maturity It takes Wisteria 3–5 years to form a framework and settle down before putting on a good display of bloom.

Lifespan 60 years plus – given care and good management.

Other varieties *W. s.* 'Alba'. A splendid white flowered form.

Uses Spectacular when covering and decorating large expanses of walls, pergolas and arches. It is also possible to use trained forms as specimen standards, as focal points or for flanking entrances.

Planting Wisteria strongly resents root disturbance so use only pot-grown plants. Set out in autumn or spring. Allow a minimum 15–20ft(4–6m) spread for wall plants, and an 8ft(2.5m) spread for standards.

Position Needs a warm, sunny, sheltered site with a south or west aspect.

Soil A moist, well-drained, moderately fertile medium loam is best. Not for very sandy, very alkaline or heavy clay soils.

Propagation Peg down layers in May. Only propagate from heavy flowering climbers.

Treatment Train up a support immediately after planting to ensure the formation of a good framework. Keep well watered.

Pruning PG3. Shorten back sideshoots to 5 or 7 leaves in July, so leaving a short stub. In February cut back each of these stubs to 2 or 3 buds.

Problems Chlorosis is likely to be a problem if grown on alkaline soils. Aphids and red spider mites may attack.